Nature Spirituality

Nature Spirituality

Praying with Wind, Water, Earth, Fire

Mark G. Boyer

RESOURCE *Publications* • Eugene, Oregon

NATURE SPIRITUALITY
Praying with Wind, Water, Earth, Fire

Copyright © 2013 Mark G. Boyer. All rights reserved. Except for brief quotations in critical publications or reviews, no part of this book may be reproduced in any manner without prior written permission from the publisher. Write: Permissions, Wipf and Stock Publishers, 199 W. 8th Ave., Suite 3, Eugene, OR 97401.

Resource Publications
An Imprint of Wipf and Stock Publishers
199 W. 8th Ave., Suite 3
Eugene, OR 97401

www.wipfandstock.com

ISBN 13: 978-1-62564-434-3

Manufactured in the U.S.A.

All the Scripture quotations contained herein, except for the books of Wisdom and Sirach, are from the Contemporary English Version, copyright © 1991, 1992, 1995 by American Bible Society, 1865 Broadway, New York, NY 10023. Used by permission. All rights reserved.

The Scripture quotations from the books of Wisdom and Sirach, are from the New Revised Standard Version Bible: Catholic Edition, copyright © 1993 and 1989 by the Division of Christian Education of the National Council of the Churches of Christ in the U.S.A. Used by permission. All rights reserved.

Dedicated to
my elementary and high school teachers
in St. Joachim School,
Old Mines, Missouri, 1956–1968

The Father's kingdom is spread out upon the earth, and people do not see it.

—Gospel of Thomas 113:2

Contents

	Introduction	xi
1	**Wind**	1

    Mighty Wind
    Breath of Life
    No Breath
    Calm Winds
    Spirit Like Wind
    Grass Blown by Wind
    Four Winds
    Saving Wind
    Food on Wind
    Not in the Wind
    Life-like Wind
    Drying Wind
    Saving Wind
    Scattered like Wind
    Swept Away by Wind
    Storehouse of Wind
    Hair in the Wind
    All Breathe Alike
    Wind Breathing Life
    Wind-tossed Ship

2	**Water**	31

    Separate Waters
    Four Rivers
    Great Flood
    Water from Rock
    Crossing the Jordan

Contents

    Dew on the Wool
    Rain Stopped
    Water and Fire
    Divided Water
    Washed Clean
    Snow and Ice
    Well of Victory
    Rejected Water
    Clean Water
    Temple Water
    Split Water
    Water into Wine
    Water and Spirit
    Living Water
    Water and Blood

3   Earth   63

    Earth Created
    People of Earth
    Tower of Earth
    Altar of Earth
    Swallowed by Earth
    Wagon of Earth
    Promise of Earth
    Slaves of Earth
    God of Earth
    Temple of Earth
    Earth's Foundations
    Dust and Ashes
    Potter Works Earth
    Earth Wears Out
    New Earth
    Jesus In the Earth
    Lifted Above Earth
    Earthen Jar
    Earthen Vessel
    Earthquake

4   **Fire**   99

Raining Fire
Fiery Sacrifice
Burning Bush
Flaming Fire
Pillar of Fire
Burned Offering
Consumed by Fire
Fire from God
Fiery Chariot and Horses
Purifying Fire
Walk through Fire
King of Fire
Fiery Human
Saved in Fire
Destroying Fire
Baptized with Fire
Fiery Tongues
Fiery Anger
Hell's Fire
Post-resurrection Fire

We could say more but could never say enough;
let the final word be:
"He is the all."

—Sirach 43:27

Introduction

Take a piece of tin foil or gold foil and either go to a window where the sun is shining through or go outside. Collect the beams of light on the foil and watch them dance around. Shake the foil in the sunlight. That's what God is like—shining from shook foil. At least that's what the famous poet Gerard Manly Hopkins wrote in his poem called "God's Grandeur." He said, "The world is charged with the grandeur of God. It will flame out, like shining from shook foil."

In this book I presume that there is a Holy One who desires to "flame out, like shining from shook foil," a God who wants to enter into relationship with people, us, through any and all ways imaginable. That God wants to disclose to us who the Mighty One is, so we can share, insofar as a human being can share, in "Godness," grace, divinity.

The presence of the Divine is everywhere. That is both a comfort and a challenge. We are consoled to know that God is with us, but being human we need a sign, something to touch, see, hear, taste, smell. We need something of the ordinary to name the non-touchable, invisible, unable-to-be-heard, tasteless, odorless God's presence with us. So, we employ metaphors, figures of speech which literally denote one kind of object in place of another, to suggest a likeness or analogy. In this book, the metaphors we will use for God are the four elements of nature for the Greeks: wind, water, earth, and fire.

By reflecting on our human experiences of the elements and in relationship with the experiences of others as narrated in the Bible, we will discover God flaming out, like shining from shook foil, in our own lives. God flames out or reveals the Holy One's self metaphorically in wind, water, earth, and fire.

Traditional theology refers to God as being both immanent and transcendent. God is immanent, with us, available to our senses through the elements. And yet, simultaneously, God is not with us and not available to our senses through the elements. They are metaphors which give us but a

Introduction

little taste or feel, a tantalizing smell, a few words heard, or a sighting of the Divine's presence. By reflecting on our experiences, we discover that even as we grasp or reach for God that God is grasping and reaching toward us. The Bible, from the beginning to the end, relays stories of people of the past reaching out to and being grasped by God. Indeed, the Bible is but one long, hyphenated word for God revealing the divine presence through the elements.

God's accessibility through our human senses pushes us to articulate our experiences, much like the biblical authors wrote about theirs. Like them, we use metaphors, bridges which permit God to come to us and we to go to God. God is like wind, water, earth, and fire, and yet God is not any of those. By taking time to reflect on the elements as bridges from God to us and from us to God, we can get glimpses of the Holy One's immanence which can help us to understand God's transcendence. We find ourselves caught in the middle—standing on the bridge in the midst of the divine mystery.

To say this differently, we begin with the human signs of the elements, observing how they unfold, speak, smell, taste, and feel, and we're drawn across the bridge to encounter the divine on the other side. The meeting is usually short because we can take only so much of divine revelation at one time. So, we hurry back to our side, refreshed but desiring more.

The Elements

We begin our reflections with the element of wind. It shakes the branches of the evergreens, makes the fallen leaves rustle across the yard, and carries dust for miles. In its angry forms it launches gusts and tornados and hurricanes. On a hot day, as a breeze it cools us. Wind is a metaphor for God, especially God's Spirit, who announces the divine presence, like wind ringing chimes. Indeed, the Spirit seems to be the glue that connects every thing—human or otherwise—and leaves life wherever it blows and death in its wake.

From wind we will move to water. It falls as rain, snow, and ice from clouds. It hangs in the air as fog. Filling rivers and streams, it rushes to the seas. Water, both fresh and salty, harbors life. We pump it from wells and store it in cisterns, lakes, and reservoirs. Without water we die. And yet too much water and cities are flooded, crops ruined, homes destroyed, and people left dead. God is water, the source of our life. God is an artisan well

Introduction

gushing water all over the earth. We drink from the well, and we drink grace, divinity, eternal life.

Water leads us to solid earth, another metaphor for God. We know God through the soil, which contain God's fingerprints. The sands contain God's footprints. The land is scared, marked, by the divine. Through creation we recognize the Creator. The earth is holy ground, producing mud for bricks, clay for dishes, wheat for bread, and daisies for decoration. All that is created is so much like earth that all returns to dust, like earth. All returns to that which manifests the presence of the divine.

Finally, we look at fire as a metaphor for God's presence. Standing around a camp fire, we are drawn into its light and warmth. When a restful mood is desired, we ignite a blaze in the fireplace. Fire cooks our food, heats our water, and warms our homes. Candles are eaten by fire, as well as forests and homes. God's fire sets us ablaze with an enthusiastic spirit. God's fire purifies us so that we can recognize and stand before the all-consuming divine presence.

Four-part Exercise

This book consists of exercises in fifteen-minute nature spirituality. Because we live such activity-filled lives, we have little time for the silence needed to enter into the divine mystery by contemplating one of the elements. Each of the four chapters in this book offers 20 reflections organized into four parts which will provide the reader with about a fifteen-minute reflection on God's presence using one of the four elements.

The first part of each exercise is a short quotation from Scripture. It focuses on one aspect of the topic of the chapter. The reflection, part two, explores the metaphor found in the Scripture passage for its meanings and makes some applications for today. In the journal section, part three, the reader makes connections between the biblical passage, the reflection, and his or her own life. Those connections may be written down or meditated on with the help of the questions. Once the reader is finished, the exercise is concluded with a short prayer.

The four-part process is called nature spirituality, a way of preparing the self to become aware of God's presence. Through the elements, we meet the living God and are divinized through God's gift of self, grace, to us. We are transformed, transfigured, by God. After meeting the divine, we better understand all of the circumstances of our lives, including our unique

Introduction

selves. Spirituality is the way that we are in God's presence, which emerges through our human experiences of the elements.

Never can we imagine that we can be fully who we were created to be. However, through the elements God gives us a taste, a touch, a smell, a sighting, a feel for the divine. We should be satisfied to erupt in joy at having experienced God "flaming out, like shining from shook foil" through wind, water, earth, and fire.

1

Wind

The Spirit is like the wind
that blows wherever it wants to.
You can hear the wind,
but you don't know where it comes from
or where it is going.

—John 3:8

A Mighty Wind

SCRIPTURE: On the day of Pentecost all the Lord's followers were together in one place. Suddenly there was a noise from heaven like the sound of a mighty wind! It filled the house where they were meeting (Acts 2:1–2).

REFLECTION: The Hebrew word for wind, "ruah," is translated into Greek as "pneuma." There is no adequate single word in English to render either of these words. In their own languages they are layered in meaning, sometimes referring to the movement of air, breath, or spirit. However, common to all the meanings assigned to "ruah" and "pneuma" is the divine dynamic activity by which God accomplishes what the Mighty One desires. This is the creative or giving-birth dimension of God.

The author of the Acts of the Apostles portrays God giving birth to the church through the wind. Jesus' followers are huddled together in a womb-like room. God takes control of them, filling them with the breath of enthusiasm and putting words in their mouths that they would never have dreamed of saying. They leave the security of their place of gestation and begin preaching the message of the risen Christ throughout the world. The mighty wind of God gives birth to the church.

God's use of wind to give birth is nothing new. The Genesis storyteller says that in the beginning, when God created the heavens and the earth, "The earth was barren, with no form of life; it was under a roaring ocean covered with darkness. But the Spirit of God was moving over the water" (1:2). Some Bibles say that "a mighty wind was moving over the water." The barren earth is like a woman's womb ready to give birth to life. God gives birth to everything through the mighty wind. The movement of the air, breath, makes everything alive. It is the Spirit that fecundates, animates, all of creation.

The creative wind of God appears again after the great flood. The Book of Genesis says: "God did not forget about Noah and the animals with him in the boat. So God made a wind blow, and the water started going down" (8:1). The wind dries the earth, Noah and the animals emerge from the ark, and a new creation begins. The Spirit of God has breathed life everywhere. God has given birth once again.

The wind or breath or spirit of God continues to give birth to life. The warm winds melt the snows and uncover the earth every year as creation is born anew. The control of breathing is taught to pregnant women in preparation for the birth of their children. God is a mighty wind in our lives—blowing us from one career to another, generating new ideas in our minds, filling us every second of every day with the breath of life—accomplishing what God desires.

JOURNAL: In what ways has God been a mighty wind in your life? How have you been re-created? In what ways do you perceive God filling the church with a mighty wind today?

PRAYER: Creating God, in your wisdom you have made the earth full of your creatures, which you fill with the breath of life. Send forth your Spirit to renew the face of the earth and to guide me in the ways of your Son, Jesus Christ, who is Lord for ever and ever. Amen.

Breath of Life

SCRIPTURE: The LORD God took a handful of soil and made a man. God breathed life into the man, and the man started breathing. . . . The LORD God made him fall into a deep sleep, and he took out one of the man's ribs. Then after closing the man's side, the LORD made a woman out of the rib (Genesis 2:7, 21–22).

REFLECTION: In the second story of creation, which is older than the first, God resembles a potter, sitting at the wheel, throwing clay into all types of shapes and forms. Once the clay is molded, however, God breathes on it, and it comes alive. God blows into it the breath of life, the spirit that animates it, the wind that distinguishes it from that which is dead. Once a clay figurine begins to breathe, it continues to inhale and exhale, feasting on God's Spirit, until it returns to the soil from which it was made.

Long before machines were invented to measure heartbeats and brain waves ancient cultures used breath to determine whether or not a person was still alive. A feather from the down of a fowl would be placed under the nose of an unconscious person. If the feather moved, the individual was declared to be full of spirit. If the tuft stayed in place, the breath of life had departed, and the person was dead. Since there is some moisture exhaled in the process of respiration, a mirror or other glass often was placed under an incognizant person's nose. If a fog appeared on the glass, the individual was alive. If there were no fog, death had stolen the breath of life from him or her.

The author of John's Gospel applies the Genesis metaphor of God breathing life into God's clay figures to Jesus in two ways. The author of the Fourth Gospel states: "The disciples were afraid . . . , and . . . they locked themselves in a room. Suddenly, Jesus appeared in the middle of the group. He greeted them and showed them his hands and his side. When the disciples saw the Lord, they became very happy. After Jesus had greeted them again, he said, 'I am sending you just as the Father has sent me.' Then he breathed on them and said, 'Receive the Holy Spirit'" (John 20:19–22).

First, Jesus is alive. He is full of the breath of life, the Spirit of God. He has been raised from the dead by God, who did for Jesus what God did for the first man and woman he had created: God breathed life into him. Second, Jesus breathes life into his followers, who are dead in fear and all huddled together behind locked doors. Jesus' breath is so violent that it blows open the doors and sends the disciples into the world to continue his work. They, like him, are filled with the very life of God, the Holy Spirit.

Every inhalation, every exhalation recalls the memory of God blowing breath into creation and of God re-creating in and through the resurrection of Jesus Christ. The windy Spirit of God animates all of our days and nights.

Journal: When have you been dead and God has breathed new life into you? In what ways has the Spirit animated you?

Prayer: Living God, you not only fill me with life, but you re-create me in the image of Jesus. I join everything that breathes in praising you through Christ, whom you raised from the dead and lives for ever and ever. Amen.

No Breath

Scripture: For forty days the rain poured down without stopping. And the water became deeper and deeper, until the boat started floating high above the ground. The LORD destroyed everything that breathed.

Nothing was left alive except Noah and the others in the boat (Genesis 7:17, 22–23).

Reflection: The God of the Book of Genesis who first breathes the breath of life into all of the Holy One's clay figurines also takes it away with the great flood. The spirit that animates God's creation is washed away. Only the patriarch Noah, his family, and the creatures he has captured in the boat remain filled with the wind of life.

Without breath, people are like statues waiting to be carved from a marble block. Breathing spirit-air makes persons like God. However, when they cease to live like God, their breath is removed. When sin has scared the earth, God sends the flood which turns clay figurines into mud. They no longer have distinctive shapes; they no longer have the breath of life in them.

Having the breath of life within is how we tell the difference between the true God and false gods. Idols do not breathe. They are sculptures of stone, wood, or metal, imprisoned in their temples. The real God cannot be contained in a temple or imaged in a statue. The real God is spirit. And God makes people out of what the Holy One is.

In the Hebrew Bible, Noah becomes a new first human, a pattern that will be repeated over and over again until it reaches a crescendo in Jesus of Nazareth, the Son of God, the very enfleshment of God's self. It takes a long time for people to learn how to breathe the pure spirit of God. Abraham and Sarah; Isaac and Rebekah; Jacob and Rachel, Leah, Zilpah, and Bilhah; the judges; the kings; and the prophets learn how to breathe deeply of God's Spirit. Jesus not only teaches how to inhale and exhale like God, he restores the original creation by breathing the Holy Spirit into it. Thus, God's clay figurines are restored to life through the death and resurrection of Christ.

Now, we share in this life. We are no longer without the breath of life. In fact, God has told us: "I promise every living creature that the earth and those living on it will never again be destroyed by a flood" (Genesis 9:11).

Journal: What floods have washed away your breath of life? How did God breathe new life into you? What idols do you find in the world today? How can you tell they are idols?

Prayer: Eternal God, no flood can overwhelm what you have revealed through the ages. Help me to recognize my idols as the work of human hands. Breathe new life into me as you did your Son, Jesus Christ, whom you raised from the dead. He is Lord for ever and ever. Amen.

Calm Winds

SCRIPTURE: . . . Jesus said to his disciples, "Let's cross to the east side." Suddenly a windstorm struck the lake. Waves started splashing into the boat, and it was about to sink. Jesus was in the back of the boat with his head on a pillow, and he was asleep. His disciples woke him and said, "Teacher, don't you care that we're about to drown?" Jesus got up and ordered the wind and the waves to be quiet. The wind stopped, and everything was calm (Mark 4:35, 37–39).

REFLECTION: The story of Jesus calming the wind is found in all three synoptic gospels with slight variations (Mark 4:35–41, Matthew 8:18, 23–27, Luke 8:22–25), while another calming-of-the wind story, preceded by Jesus walking on the water, is found in Mark (6:45–52), Matthew (14:22–33), and John (6:15–21). Matthew alters his Markan source by portraying Peter as walking on the water toward Jesus.

No matter which of the stories you read concerning the calming of the wind, the point remains the same. Jesus is God. The stories echo the mighty wind or "Spirit of God . . . moving over the water" in Genesis (1:2). The ancient author records: "God said, 'I command the water under the sky to come together in one place, so there will be dry ground.' And that's what happened" (Genesis 1:9). The watery, wind-driven chaos is ordered by the word of God.

Jesus manifests his divinity when he calms the winds and the waves. He, like God, gives the command and creation obeys his every word. Furthermore, the wind breathes fear into the disciples, until Jesus calms their fear. The windstorm strikes doubt into Jesus' followers, until he offers them faith. Their fear and their doubt are quieted by the one asleep on the pillow, the one who saves them from perishing.

Jesus is God manifested in the wind. He teaches his followers not to fear the wind, but to calm it. He shows them how to stand firm when doubts enter into their minds. The Son of God re-creates the world and saves it.

Just when the wind of despair over the loss of a job blows us away, our sails are filled with the new hope of job prospects. As money is tight and we are down to our last few dollars and creditors are buffeting our bank account, an unexpected gift arrives by way of air mail. After having a bad day of squalls, the evening becomes an occasion for sharing the breath of life with family and friends. Each experience of wind stirs us up and then calms us down. We are re-created as Jesus, God manifested in the wind, saves us.

JOURNAL: What have been some of your recent experiences of being in a windstorm? In what ways were you afraid? How were you calmed? How was Jesus manifesting God in the wind?

PRAYER: Almighty God, you command and raise the stormy wind, which lifts up the waves of the sea and melts the courage of people. But when I cry to you in trouble, you bring me out from distress. You make the storm be still, and you hush the waves of the sea. Thanks be to you through Jesus Christ now and for ever. Amen.

Spirit Like Wind

SCRIPTURE: [Jesus said to Nicodemus:] "Only God's Spirit gives new life. The Spirit is like the wind that blows wherever it wants to. You can hear the wind, but you don't know where it comes from or where it is going" (John 3:8).

REFLECTION: During the spring and the summer, while mowing the lawn or working in the garden, we hear the leaves of the trees rustle and we conclude that it is the wind. In the fall the leaves flutter from the trees in the cool breeze and march across the lawn to the corner of the fence where they are banked into piles by the wind. The moaning and whistling of the winter wind cuts right through our coats and scarves. It whispers through the evergreens and shakes the snow from their branches.

No matter what the season, we do not know from where the wind comes and we do not know to where it goes. We might see a line on a weather map indicating the jet stream, but that merely indicates the pattern of the wind; the line is not the wind. We might see a windsock filled with air at the airport, but it is not the wind. Observing a banner and hearing it flutter in the breeze tells us there is wind blowing, but the flapping flag is not the wind.

The wind is immaterial. It cannot be contained. It cannot be captured. Its velocity can be measured, but the next gust may be greater or lesser than the previous one. The author of the Hebrew Bible (Old Testament) Book of Ecclesiastes writes, "The wind blows south, the wind blows north; round and round it blows over and over again" (1:6). Then, he adds, ". . . Everything is just as senseless as chasing the wind" (1:14). The wind can never be caught.

That is why the author of John's Gospel portrayed Jesus as comparing the Spirit of God to the wind. God, immaterial being, is manifested in the wind. Yet, the Spirit of God cannot be contained or captured. It cannot even be measured. It is senseless to chase after God's Spirit, since it is God who, like the wind, finds us. God rustles us. God pushes us to march across the world. God whistles through our lives and whispers in our silences. And when God does so, we are filled, bloated, by the Spirit and born again and again and again. We know from whom the Spirit comes and to whom it goes, but, like the wind, it cannot be held for even a moment.

JOURNAL: When have you recently experienced the windy Spirit of God? Were you rustled, pushed, or whispered to? How were you filled? In what ways did you experienced being born again?

PRAYER: Mighty God, you give us snow like wool; you scatter frost like ashes; you hurl hail like crumbs. Then, you make the wind blow and melt the snow, frost, and hail. Send your word to me. May you be praised by all people through Jesus Christ now and for ever. Amen.

Grass Blown By Wind

SCRIPTURE: . . . Jesus spoke to the crowds about John: "What sort of person did you go out into the desert to see? Was he like tall grass blown about by the wind?" (Matthew 11:7)

REFLECTION: With some slight variations, Jesus' speech about John the Baptist (Matthew 11:7–11) also occurs in Luke's Gospel (7:24–28).

Because the monologue is not found in Mark's Gospel, biblical scholars conclude that it comes from the unique source used by both the author of Matthew's Gospel and the author of Luke's Gospel called Q (for "Quelle," a German word meaning "source").

Posed in question form, Jesus tells the crowd that John was like wind blowing over the tall grass and bending it with the gentle breeze of his hand. John the Baptizer wasn't dressed like a king. Indeed, "John wore clothes made of camel's hair. He had a leather strap around his waist . . ." (Matthew 3:4). His role was that of prophet—to wake up people—and messenger—to announce what God was doing. To put it simply, John was God's wind blowing through the tall grass of God's people and bending them according to God's ways.

John the Baptist became a mighty wind of God, baptizing with water, but declaring that there was a greater one coming who would baptize with the Holy Spirit. That is why Jesus speaks of John as being greater than anyone ever born on earth. And yet the least person in God's kingdom is greater than John, because the Baptist only fulfilled his role.

John the Baptists continue to blow through our tall grass today. Some of them bend us to see the poor and the homeless who must be fed and sheltered. Some of them blow through our emotions with pictures of malnourished children, refugees, and immigrants from worn-torn countries and move us to help them. Our tall grass of pride is often bent by the wind of one who is much better at what we do than we are, and we are forced to learn from him or her. In every instance, the wind is God manifested as a John who blows us about until God gets us where God wants us to be.

JOURNAL: What "prophet" or "messenger" have you recently experienced as a mighty wind in your life? How were you bent? How did you respond? How was God present to you in the wind of that person?

PRAYER: Eternal God, you make the clouds your chariot and you ride on the wings of the wind. Attune me to the winds of your messengers that I may sing your praise as long as live through your Son, Jesus Christ, who is Lord for ever and ever. Amen.

Four Winds

SCRIPTURE: "... I [, John,] saw four angels. Each one was standing on one of the earth's four corners. The angels held back the four winds, so that no wind would blow on the earth or on the sea or on any tree" (Revelation 7:1).

REFLECTION: In some ancient cosmologies, the earth, the center of a three-storied universe, is pictured as a flat rectangle or square. When God sends the winds from the four sides of the rectangle—north, south, east, and west—they are the good winds that do God's will.

The prophet Zechariah relays this information when he narrates one of his visions. An angel tells him, "These are the four winds of heaven, and now they are going out, after presenting themselves to the Lord of all the earth" (6:5). The angel singles out the north wind, telling the prophet, "Those that have gone to the country in the north will do what the LORD's Spirit wants them to do there" (6:8).

When the winds come from the four corners of the rectangle or square, they are sent for destructive purposes, as portrayed in the Book of Revelation. The angels hold back the four winds, while God's chosen people are marked or sealed. Then, the stormy winds are set free to damage the earth.

Such a cosmology fell apart once scientists discovered that the earth is not a rectangle or a square, but a sphere. Good winds and harmful winds come from all directions. The north wind during the winter can cause as much damage with the ice, snow, sleet, and below-zero temperatures it brings as does the south wind in summer with its tornados, hurricanes, and lightning storms. While the ancient understanding of the shape of the earth is no longer applicable, there is something universal to the four directions of the winds. Modern people still think in terms of north, south, east, and west.

The four winds is a way to speak about the all-encompassing and infinite God. The Holy One surrounds the earth and its people with the wind, with God's very self, the Spirit of God. When the wind blows or when it is quiet, God wraps the planet in God's love. The four directions of the wind reflect the unendingness of God. Just like east has no beginning or ending point, God is without beginning and without end. The wind is God breathing on the earth.

Nature Spirituality

Journal: Do you conceive of the earth more as a rectangle or square or as a sphere? How does your conception affect your use of north, south, east, and west? In what ways have you experienced God as wind?

Prayer: All-powerful God, you make the clouds rise at the end of the earth and you bring out the wind from your storehouse. May I never cease to praise your all-encompassing love revealed through your Son, Jesus Christ, who is Lord for ever and ever. Amen.

Saving Wind

Scripture: The LORD said to Moses, ". . . Hold your walking stick over the sea. The water will open up and make a road where [the people] can walk through on dry ground." Moses stretched his arm over the sea, and the LORD sent a strong east wind that blew all night until there was dry land where the water had been. The sea opened up, and the Israelites walked through on dry land with a wall of water on each side (Exodus 14:16, 21–22).

Reflection: The Israelites were backed into a corner. Following Moses' lead, they had made a successful escape from Egyptian slavery and were on the road to freedom when they found themselves with the sea before them and the pharaoh of Egypt and his army behind them. The hope of freedom was quickly turning into the despair of defeat.

God, however, had other plans, which involved the east wind. It comes from the east because the east is the place of the sunrise and the "location" of good and God. It echoes the story surrounding the Genesis garden, "which was in the east" (2:8). The Hebrew Bible (Old Testament) Book of Exodus does not portray the crossing of the Sea of Reeds as does Cecil B. DeMille in his famous epic "The Ten Commandments." In Exodus, the water does not part into twelve-foot-high stacks of jello! The east wind is sent by God to dry up a portion of a marshy area which can be crossed on foot, but not in chariots.

Once Israel begins to trek through the mud, the Egyptian army follows. The writer states, "Their chariot wheels got stuck, and it was hard for them to move" (Exodus 14:25). However, the people of Israel walk on and cross through the Sea of Reeds. God saves Israel. The east wind is the means of God's salvation. It does the Holy One's will, just as God hopes the band of run-away slaves will do. The Israelites march through the mud of slavery to the solid ground of freedom. The wind creates a boundary, separating the Israelites from the Egyptians. The wind's work provides Israel with salvation. The east wind is the saving presence of God.

JOURNAL: When have you been backed into a corner with no visible escape route? How did you get out? What east wind blew through your life? How did God save you?

PRAYER: Merciful God, you are gracious, slow to anger, and abounding in steadfast love. Lead me from the slavery of sin to the freedom of one in Jesus Christ, your Son, who lives and reigns for ever and ever. Amen.

Food on Wind

SCRIPTURE: . . . The LORD sent a strong wind that blew quails in from the sea until Israel's camp was completely surrounded with birds, piled up about three feet high for miles in every direction (Numbers 11:31).

REFLECTION: Perspective, the point from which we see something, is an important consideration when it comes to understanding biblical stories, especially the account of the quails. From a scientific point of view, the quails make an annual migration across the Sinai Peninsula in the spring and the fall. If they were caught in a storm with strong winds, they would have to fly near the ground and take short jaunts. Thus, they could be captured easily by the people. From the point of view of the author of the Hebrew Bible (Old Testament) Book of Numbers, the quails were a gift from God, who cared enough for his hungry people to provide food for them.

As the story is narrated, the Israelites' abundant food came on the wings of the wind. What is implied is not only the physical food that is driven into Israel's camp, but also God as food. The "strong wind" is the source of their food, and the "strong wind" is God. Under the appearance of quails-driven-by-the-wind the Mighty One feeds people with God's self.

The Holy One had already rescued them from Egyptian slavery. Now, they eat a feast provided by the windy hand of God.

The LORD continues to feed people through the wind. Daily, we are fed with experiences driven into the camp of our lives by God's "strong wind." A friend stops to say hello and share his or her pain and suffering. We listen in respectful silence after which the correct words to say seem to come to us on the wind of the friend's breathing. God just fed us, and we shared our food with another.

Maybe we are contemplating a decision between two good actions. At first we can't make up our minds concerning the direction we should take. After asking for guidance from the divine wind of the Spirit, we wake up or step into the shower or open the door and the decision pops into our minds. The wind blew food into our camp, and the food was God.

Parents often struggle with their teenagers, wanting them to do well in high school so that they can get into a good college. However, sometimes young men and women are not ready for learning or they have their sights set in a different direction or they prefer to do things their own way. As parents give up their dreams for their children and own the dreams their children have for themselves, they find a mighty wind has been blowing through their camp and left lots of food for thought.

No matter what the experience we may have, if food is involved, we can be sure that God is feeding us. God's mighty wind piles nourishment all around us.

JOURNAL: What have been some of your recent experiences of being fed by God? What was the wind that brought you the food? How plentiful was it? How did you eat of God?

PRAYER: All-caring God, you sent food in abundance to your people when they called to you in their hunger. Fill me with your Spirit that I may know your will and do it faithfully. Hear my prayer through Jesus Christ. Amen.

Not in the Wind

SCRIPTURE: [Elijah] . . . reached Mount Sinai, the mountain of God, and he spent the night there in a cave. "Go out and stand on the mountain," the LORD [said]. "I want you to see me when I pass by." All at once, a strong wind shook the mountain and shattered the rocks. But the LORD was not in the wind. Next, there was an earthquake, but he LORD was not in the earthquake. Then there was a fire, but the LORD was not in the fire. Finally, there was a gentle breeze, and when Elijah heard it, he covered his face with his coat. He went out and stood at the entrance to the cave (1 Kings 19:8–9, 11–13).

REFLECTION: The story of Elijah's experience on Mount Sinai negates our understanding of God as wind, earth, water, and fire. It has to do so because while it is true to say that God is wind, earth, water, and fire, it is just as true to say that God is none of these. However, even the writer of the Hebrew Bible (Old Testament) First Book of Kings knows that it is impossible to write about God without using some material manifestation of the divine. So, the "strong wind" that God is not gives way to the "gentle breeze" that God is. Only the degree of the blast serves as a distinguishing characteristic.

Elijah has been driven by the wind of God's disloyal people to the refuge of the Holy One's dwelling place, Mount Sinai. He was running scared, propelled by the wrong wind. And that is what God makes Elijah understand by permitting him "to see" God. The Mighty One displays God's self not as a strong wind or earth or water or fire, but as a gentle breeze, which calms the prophet's fear and sends him back on his mission, propelled by the strong wind of God's plans.

When we run from our fears, like Elijah, we are simultaneously driven forward by a mighty wind other than that of God and lose sight of our mission. Fear of losing a job in an age of downsizing can drive us to drinking too much alcohol. Fear of failure in school can propel students into escape through drug use. A whole city can become paralyzed with fear in the face of gangs.

Somewhere on the mountain of fear we climb we discover that God is not in the strong wind of fear that has been motivating us. In fact, the Mighty One is not in the earthquake or the fire, but it is a gentle, calming breeze that displays the presence of the divine. The gentle breeze of God helps us know we've taken the wrong road. Once we find our way, the mighty wind picks up again.

Nature Spirituality

JOURNAL: What fears have sent you in a direction not in God's plan for you? How did you not find God in the strong wind blowing you into fear? What gentle breeze helped you discover that you needed to go back? How are you like Elijah?

PRAYER: Mighty God, in my fear I cry to you for help and you hear my voice. Grant that I may always delight in your presence and praise you through your Son, Jesus Christ, who lives and reigns with you and the Holy Spirit, one God, for ever and ever. Amen.

Life Like Wind

SCRIPTURE: [Job said:] I beg you, God, don't forget! My life is just a breath, and trouble lies ahead. I will vanish from sight, and no one, including you, will ever see me again. I will disappear in the grave or vanish from sight like a passing cloud (Job 7:7–9).

REFLECTION: At first it might be depressing to summarize life as a single breath, as Job does. But as we age, we come to know the truth of Job's meditation. If we stand back and take a look at the big picture, we realize that our lives can be measured as breaths. Our days are numbered and pass quickly. They run out, we are buried, and return to dust.

The author of the Hebrew Bible (Old Testament) Book of Ecclesiastes also reflected on this truth. In reference to people who get rich, he writes: "They came into this world naked, and when they die, they will be just as naked. They can't take anything with them, and they won't have anything to show for all their work. That's terribly unfair. They leave the world just as they came into it. They gather nothing from running after the wind" (5:15–16). It might be unfair, but that's the way it is: Life is only a breath, or in Ecclesiastes' words, "chasing the wind" (1:17).

Instead of focusing on the depression that this reflection could cause with its emphasis on the shortness of life, we should pay more attention to the measure of life as a breath. God is breath. God is wind. One breath of God fills our lungs with enough air for a lifetime. We are permeated by the Divine who blows the breath of life into us. From God's perspective, when we measure our lives as but a single breath, we are bursting with a share in the existence, the being, that fills all things.

JOURNAL: Explore your feelings about the shortness of your life. Are you depressed, happy, or somewhere in between? In what ways have you experienced the wind of God's breath that filled you with divine life? How are you connected to all things, including God?

PRAYER: Eternal God, you make my heart glad; my soul rejoices. You fill me with the breath of life, and, through Jesus Christ, you have revealed the path of life. May all praise be to you, Father, Son, and Holy Spirit, now and for ever. Amen.

Drying Wind

SCRIPTURE: The Lord will dry up the arm of the Red Sea near Egypt, and he will send a scorching wind to divide the Euphrates River into seven streams that anyone can step across. Then for his people who survive, there will be a good road . . . , just as there was a good road for their ancestors when they left Egypt (Isaiah 11:15–16).

REFLECTION: The Euphrates is the largest river of western Asia, running about 1,700 miles in length from its source in the Armenian highlands to its mouth in the Persian Gulf. In the ancient world it was to Mesopotamia what the Nile River was to Egypt. Knowing these facts is what makes the prophet Isaiah's words so amazing. The prophet said that the wind would be so dry that it would divide the Euphrates into seven streams which could be crossed with no difficulty.

Isaiah is writing for the Israelites, who were prisoners of war in Babylon, a city located on the left bank of the Euphrates River. The Jewish captives were deported to Babylon, the capital of Babylonia, after the fall of Jerusalem in 586 BCE. In order to return to their own land, they would have to cross the Euphrates, like they had to cross the Sea of Reeds when they left Egypt.

Isaiah says that they will cross the Euphrates, like they once crossed the Sea of Reeds, because God will send a scorching wind which will dry the river into smaller streams. Just like "the LORD sent a strong east wind that blew all night until there was dry land where the water had been" (Exodus 14:21) for the Israelites to march through the Red Sea, so will a new exodus take place when the Jews leave Babylon and cross the seven wind-cut streams of the great Euphrates.

In our own time, the wind continues to dry up the great rivers that we need to cross. When one person respects another enough to tell the absolute truth, he or she has crossed a river divided into streams by God's wind. Giving another human being what is honestly due him or her means that we may have to cross the great river of prejudice, but God will divide it with the drying wind so that it is not as difficult as we first surmised. When parents speak to their children openly about drugs, alcohol, and sex, they cross major rivers which can be made into small streams by God's scorching wind.

Every waterway we cross is divided or dried up by the divine wind. That means every time we cross a river in our lives, we escape from slavery to freedom, like Israel once crossed through the Sea of Reeds and through the Euphrates.

Journal: What great rivers have you recently crossed in your life? How were they divided into small streams by God's scorching wind? What did you find on the other side?

Prayer: Mighty God, once you saved your people by drying the Sea of Reeds. You delivered them from the hand of their enemy, and you saved them. Help me to cross every river that separates me from my brothers and sisters. Save me through Jesus Christ, who is Lord for ever and ever. Amen.

Sowing Wind

Scripture: If you scatter wind instead of wheat, you will harvest a whirlwind and have no wheat (Hosea 8:7ab).

Reflection: The prophet Hosea compares the sowing of wind to idolatry, a sin into which the Israelites repeatedly fell. Since idols are not real, worship of them is like scattering wind. When time for the harvest comes, only a whirlwind can be reaped. Or, in other words, if you sow wind, you harvest wind.

However, if the sower scatters wheat seeds, he or she will glean wheat at harvest time. Worshiping God brings benefits to Israel.

The prophet Isaiah used a similar image to describe the suffering of the people. He writes that when God punished the people, they turned and prayed to him. Because of what he did to them, they suffered like a woman about to give birth. But instead of having a child, their terrible pain produced only wind" (cf. Isaiah 26:16–18a). Without God, suffering has no meaning. It is like being pregnant with wind. Once the labor pains are endured, there is nothing to show for them.

What both prophets fail to recognize is that wind reveals the Spirit of God. The windy Spirit permeates everything and fills it with life. People's suffering is fruitful. Hosea portrays God as saying: "Israel, I can't let you go. I can't give you up. I just can't do it. My feelings for you are much too strong. I am the Holy God—not merely some human . . . (11:8acd, 9a). Likewise, Isaiah, speaking for God, declares: "Your people will rise to life! Tell them to leave their graves and celebrate with shouts. You refresh the earth like morning dew; you give life to the dead" (26:19).

Sow a few ideas about the equality in dignity of all people, and watch the Spirit whip up a whirlwind. Enter into the travail of self-knowledge and you give birth to a spirituality of the wind. Learn how to die, and you'll reap the wind of the Spirit of life; you will give birth to that which gave birth to you. The wind is the presence of God.

Journal: When have you recently sowed wind and reaped wind or entered into labor pains and given birth to wind? At first did you think that your efforts were futile? How did you come to see that you had really reaped the Spirit or given birth to the Spirit of God?

Prayer: Lord God, you never cease to make my suffering fruitful. May all that I sow in tears become a harvest of joy. I ask this through Jesus Christ, your Son, who lives with you and the Holy Spirit, for ever and ever. Amen.

Scattered Like Wind

SCRIPTURE: Everyone who hates you will be terribly disgraced; those who attack will vanish into thin air. You will look around for those brutal enemies, but you won't find them because they will be gone. I am the LORD you God. I am holding your hand, so don't be afraid. I am here to help you. A strong wind will scatter them in all directions. Then you will celebrate and praise me, your LORD, the holy God of Israel (Isaiah 41:11–13, 16).

REFLECTION: As soon as one person or a group of people are labeled "the enemy," we have division. "The enemy" may be someone who seeks to injure us, such as a person with a knife or gun; to overthrow us, such as causing a loss of a job or the office we hold in a group; or to confound us, by proposing ideas which threaten us in some manner. "The enemy" can be something harmful to us, such as diseases or viruses. For some people, death is "the enemy," because it robs them of life. In world politics, "the enemy" is a military adversary seeking to conquer us with hostility or force. Naming "the enemy" immediately draws a line down the center of the playground and declares that there are two sides.

What happens when "the enemy" is not named? What happens if no line is drawn down the middle of the playground? If we begin with the unity of all creation in God, there is no division. Divisiveness disappears into thin air. The wind scatters the enemy in all directions. God, you see, is not interested in dividing creation, but in keeping it united. People make enemies, either by declaring themselves the aggressor or by naming the other to be the adversary.

God's wind scatters the enemy, eliminating division, because the wind is the Spirit of God. The strong wind can change direction without notice. God can change people without them being aware. The jet stream of imminent war can be blown away by the undercurrents of peace. The hostility between two people can vanish with a breath of fresh air. An illness can be converted into energy by the currents of attitudinal change. And "the enemy"—no matter who or what he, she, it may be—will scatter when God blasts the windy Spirit of unity throughout the universe.

JOURNAL: Who or what have you labeled "the enemy" in the past few months? What types of divisiveness resulted? How did God's windy Spirit scatter the divisions and restore unity? In what ways have you been changed?

PRAYER: Mighty God, you have created all in unity. Remove all that divides from my life. Living in your Spirit, I praise you through Jesus Christ, who is Lord for ever and ever. Amen.

Swept Away By Wind

SCRIPTURE: When disaster comes, the LORD will tell you people of Jerusalem, "I am sending a windstorm from the desert—not a welcome breeze. And it will sweep you away as punishment for your sins. Look! The enemy army swoops down like an eagle; their cavalry and chariots race faster than storm clouds blown by the wind." Then you will answer, "We are doomed!" But Jerusalem, there is still time for you to be saved. Wash the evil from your hearts and stop making sinful plans, before a message of disaster arrives . . . (Jeremiah 4:11–15a).

REFLECTION: Repeatedly, the prophet Jeremiah employs the image of the windstorm to depict the sweeping away of the Israelites from Jerusalem to Babylon. The prophet records God stating: "I will scatter you, just as the desert wind blows husks from grain tossed in the air. I won't change my mind. I, the LORD, have spoken" (Jeremiah 13:24–25a); "When your enemies attack, I will scatter you like dust blown by an eastern wind" (18:17a); "Your leaders will be swept away by the wind, and the nations you trusted will be captured and dragged to a foreign country" (22:22b).

"To be swept away by the wind" implies the use of a broom. We use a broom to sweep the floor, the porch, the sidewalk. Just like the broom scatters the dust through the air, so will the people of Jerusalem be swept away to captivity because of their sins—at least that is how Jeremiah interpreted the signs of his time.

God is always in the process of sweeping away and scattering sin with the wind, the Spirit. Sometimes that means that we have to go into captivity because we are too close to our own sinfulness to recognize it. Once we are blown away, we can see how much sweeping God needed to do with the Holy One's broom of Spirit. We can return once the dust settles.

Sometimes our captivity consists of getting away to a retreat. If we are honest with ourselves, we have to make or take time to get away to reflect for a few days. At first we are lost, having been blown in with no plans and nothing to do. But the Holy One has swept us there and remains occupied with scattering all that is not authentically us, like the wind blows away the husks from the grain. Once we are "husked," we go home filled with the windy Spirit of God.

Taking time for ourselves every day is a type of captivity. In order to take the time to pray, to be with people we really love, to read, to work, etc. means that we have to give up some other activities. We must create a captivity for ourselves as the wind sweeps away everything else. Some people call the process prioritizing, but God calls it being swept away by the Spirit.

What the storm wind of God teaches us is that going to a foreign country does not have to be a negative experience. In our captivity we can grow in Spirit and return home renewed.

JOURNAL: Into what type of captivity have you been pushed by God's stormwind? How did you grow? What needed to be swept away from your life by God's wind?

PRAYER: Lord, send the wind storm of your Holy Spirit into my life that I might be swept to where you need me. Bring me home renewed through Jesus Christ, your Son, who lives and reigns with you for ever and ever. Amen.

Storehouse of Wind

SCRIPTURE: God used his wisdom and power to create the earth and spread out the heavens. The waters in the heavens roar at his command. He makes clouds appear; he sends the wind from his storehouse and makes lightning flash in the rain (Jeremiah 51:15–16).

REFLECTION: A storehouse is a building used for a cache of goods. In it is found an abundant supply of whatever is placed in it. A storehouse is like a pantry, whose shelves are filled with items of food. A storehouse is like a freezer, whose shelves contain package after package of frozen foods. A storehouse is like a closet, in which can be found plenty of shoes, pants, shirts, blouses, skirts, and dresses.

Ancient people portrayed God as having a storehouse above the heavens. Their cosmology consisted of a three-leveled universe. On the first level, heaven, God lived. People lived on level two, the earth. And the dead lived in level three, under the earth. The wind came from God's repository above the heavens. God opened up the storehouse of wind and it blew over the earth, bringing clouds, lightning, and rain.

Twice the prophet Jeremiah refers to God's storehouse of wind. The first time, it is in direct address to God: ". . . You send the winds from your storehouse . . ." (10:13). The second reference occurs in the midst of a prayer of praise declaring what God does: ". . . He sends the wind from his storehouse . . ." (51:16). Considering that wind is a manifestation of God, we understand that the storehouse of wind is the Holy One in God's self. The Mighty One sends God's self or Spirit from the warehouse which never needs to be restocked.

God's pantry of Spirit is never depleted. We can go to it and receive all that we need. If we are seeking a path for our lives, we can ask God to send the wind from the storehouse to drive us where we need to walk. Do you need help in solving a moral dilemma? Ask for some wind from God's repository and let it blow you toward a solution. Sometimes our prayer becomes dry and routine. If we ask for some provisions of Spirit from God's storehouse, we will be filled with new life.

God's storehouse is always stocked with wind. God's storehouse is always full of Spirit. When we are in need, we have only to ask and God freely shares from God's abundance, from God's very self.

Journal: What provisions have you recently requested from God's storehouse? How did the wind of the Spirit help you? In what ways was God sharing God's self with you?

Prayer: Creator God, by your word you made the heaves and the earth and all they contain. From your storehouse send the Holy Spirit to be my counselor and guide. I ask this through Jesus Christ, who is Lord for ever and ever. Amen.

Nature Spirituality

Hair In the Wind

SCRIPTURE: The LORD said: Ezekiel, son of man, get a sharp sword and use it to cut off your hair and beard. Weight the hair and divide it into three equal piles. . . . Burn one pile of your hair. . . . Chop up the second pile and let the small pieces of hair fall . . . . Throw the third pile into the wind . . . . So tell the people of Jerusalem: A third of you will die here in Jerusalem from disease or starvation. Another third will be killed in war. And I will scatter the last third of you in every direction . . . (Ezekiel 5:1–2, 7a, 12).

REFLECTION: A sacrament is a sign which effects what it signifies. The sign, a person or thing, represents in a material form what is taking place in a spiritual realm. Thus, for example, flowing water (matter) serves as a sign of the Holy One sharing God's self with us as grace (spirit). By immersing a person in flowing water, we declare that God is pouring God's life into that individual.

Signs can be monovalent, indicating only one effect, or polyvalent, pointing toward many effects. In the example just given, water is monovalent. But, if we consider some of water's other characteristics, such as its ability to wash, to destroy, and to quench thirst, we see that it is polyvalent. Water can wash a person clean of evil desires, it can destroy sin, and it can quench our thirst for God.

Ezekiel uses human hair as a type of sacrament. He cuts off his hair and beard, signs of strength and dignity, and becomes a sign of humility and degradation. The prophet stands bald as a melon before the people of Israel and signifies their fate, what will happen to them in the fifth century BCE. One third of the people is like the one third of hair that is burned; they will die from disease and starvation in Jerusalem. A second third is like the second third of hair that is chopped up; they will be killed in the war waged by their enemies. The last third is like the last third of the hair thrown into the wind; they will be scattered across the earth and exiled to Babylon.

Being aware that the text of the prophet was most likely influenced by and written after Jerusalem was destroyed by the Babylonians, it effected what it signified. But it is only from the perspective of the return to Jerusalem after seventy years of captivity that the third part of the hair scattered in the wind can offer hope. Indeed, if the Jews had not returned to Jerusalem, Ezekiel's words would have been borne away on the wind.

The hair scattered in the wind offers hope because not only is God the agent of the scattering, but God is also the gatherer. At least that is how Ezekiel sees the big picture and makes sense out of the fall of Jerusalem, the exile, and the return to Jerusalem. The wind of God's Spirit scatters and gathers, dividing and uniting. Both are necessary in the spiritual life.

Sometimes we need to be scattered. For example, when our focus on today's project is so concentrated that we do not see or hear anyone but ourselves, we need to be scattered. When we become mired in the mud of our daily routines, we need some scattering. Even intense personal relationships often need to be scattered. The wind blows through us and effects the scattering so that we can be gathered anew. We are able to see others again. We are freed from so many "must do" things each day. We appreciate the one we love even more.

JOURNAL: When have you been recently scattered like hair in the wind. How were you bald and humiliated? What gathering did the windy Spirit of God effect in your life?

PRAYER: Saving God, you always hear my prayer. Scatter and gather me that I may do your will. In the abundance of your steadfast love, answer me through Jesus Christ, my Lord. Amen.

All Breathe Alike

SCRIPTURE: Like animals we breathe and die, and we are no better off than they are. It just doesn't make sense. All living creatures go to the same place. We are made from earth, and we return to the earth. Who really knows if our spirits go up and the spirits of animals go down into the earth? (Ecclesiastes 3:19–21)

REFLECTION: The author of the Hebrew Bible (Old Testament) Book of Ecclesiastes brings together all living creatures under two categories: breath and death. Every living thing needs to breathe in order to survive. It makes no difference whether the process is inhaling oxygen and exhaling carbon dioxide, inhaling carbon dioxide and exhaling

Nature Spirituality

oxygen, or getting oxygen through water. One common denominator of all life is breath.

The other common denominator according to Ecclesiastes is death. After months of years of breathing, every living thing stops breathing, dies, and begins to decay. The process of deterioration turns the bodies of living things to dust, dirt, earth. Therefore, the conclusion is that all living things must be made from earth, since that is to what all return.

But in his wisdom the author of this biblical book notices something else that all living things have in common: spirit. He attributes spirit, that which is more than breath and death, to all that lives. From our first breath to our last one and beyond we share God's Spirit. It is a single breath of God from whom and to whom all things are. As Paul told the Romans: "Everything comes from the Lord. All things were made because of him and will return to him. Praise the Lord forever! Amen" (Romans 11:36).

JOURNAL: In what ways are you connected to all living things through breath and death? In what ways are you connected to all living things through spirit?

PRAYER: Eternal God, I will praise you as long as I live for you breathe the life of your Spirit into me. Strengthen me in hope, faith, and love until I return to you, the origin of all things. Hear my prayer through Jesus Christ. Amen.

Wind Breathing Life

SCRIPTURE: . . . I {, Ezekiel,] felt the LORD'S power take control of me, and his Spirit carried me to a valley full of bones. He then told me to say: Dry bones, listen to what the LORD is saying to you, "I, the LORD God, will put breath in you, and once gain you will live. I will wrap you with muscles and skin and breathe life into you. Then you will know that I am the LORD." The LORD said: "Ezekiel, now say to the wind, 'The LORD God commands you to blow from every direction and to breathe life into these dead bodies, so they can live again.'" As soon as I said this, the wind blew among the bodies, and they came back to life! They all stood up, and there were enough to make a large army (Ezekiel 37:1, 4–6, 9–10).

Wind

REFLECTION: Every human being at one time or another experiences a loss of enthusiasm for life. Enthusiasm dwindles because of tiredness. Boredom is often brought on by routine. To renew our lives, we will take a three-day weekend vacation or a few weeks off during the summer. We come back to life and its tasks refreshed.

The prophet Ezekiel faced the same problem. While the Israelites were in captivity in Babylon, they lost their enthusiasm for returning home to Israel and they became bored with living in Babylon. They were like dead bones, without hope. But God promised them that he would fill them with new life, a life that would be blown into them by the wind. So, Ezekiel calls upon the wind to blow from every direction and to blow life into the dead so that they could live again.

It is God who gives enthusiasm and life and spirit and breath. To demonstrate that, the prophet calls upon the wind to come from all directions. God is everywhere and fills everything. The Creator, who once blew the breath of life into the first man, not only rebuilds bones with muscles and skin, but also blows the wind through the bones and fills them with life.

Mired in boredom we are like dead bones. We need renewal. A retreat in silence for a few hours or a few days can serve to let the windy Spirit of God blow through us and bring us to life again. During a directed retreat, this writer once stood on the top of a hill and prayed his version of Ezekiel's prayer "Come, O winds, from every direction, and give me life." The leaves of the trees began to rustle and he felt the breeze against his body. And he was filled with God's life, the Spirit, the wind that blows from every direction. He left that retreat with renewed enthusiasm for his work.

JOURNAL: Identify three or four times in the past few years when you lost enthusiasm or found yourself immersed in boredom? What did you do to re-energize yourself? What wind blew through your life? How did God give your dry bones new life?

PRAYER: Lord God, I will praise you at all times because you hear the brokenhearted and save the crushed in spirit. On my last day, breathe new life into me and raise me as you did your Son, Jesus Christ, who is Lord for ever and ever. Amen.

Wind-Tossed Ship

SCRIPTURE: . . . Jonah ran from the LORD. He went to the seaport of Joppa and bought a ticket on a ship that was going to Spain. Then he got on the ship and sailed away to escape. But the LORD made a strong wind blow, and such a bad storm came up that the ship was about to be broken to pieces. All this time, Jonah was down below deck, sound asleep. The storm kept getting worse, until finally the sailors asked him, "What should we do with you to make the sea calm down?" Jonah told them, "Throw me into the sea, and it will calm down. I'm the cause of this terrible storm." Then they threw Jonah overboard, and the sea calmed down (Jonah 1:3–4, 5c, 11–12, 15).

REFLECTION: Who hasn't run away from God? We are always in the process of being stopped by the strong wind blowing against our ship, rocking and reeling, until we are tossed overboard. The strong wind is God's way of awakening us, rerouting us, and getting us to where God wants us to be. Jonah thought that he could sail away from God only to discover that God had sailed toward Jonah.

Maybe it's the boat of investment that we get into. Our stocks and bonds bring in rich dividends, but they are at the cost of exploitation of cheap labor. A strong moral wind begins to rock our consciences, and we realize that we must divest ourselves of the stocks and bonds which profit us at the cost of others.

God's wind often tosses our boat of security onto the waves of the world. Family problems appear, a job is lost to downsizing, we're overworked, a filling falls out of a tooth, the computer crashes, the report is late, etc. Our day is ruined and we are nearly capsized. But after a day of relaxation and rest and prayer, we pull the divergent pieces of our lives together again and realize that our only security is in God.

Relationships are often swept clean by God's wind. Friendships and marital relationships can become dependencies instead of freeing both parties to be more of who each is. Authenticity is difficult to maintain, but is an absolute necessity if two people are to foster each other's growth in all areas of life. As the cargo that each has accumulated is thrown overboard, individuality re-emerges and the relationship simultaneously deepens self-knowledge and love of the other. Both discover that the wind of God has expanded them.

Wind

Jonah's encounter with God's wind on the ship is also the story of our encounter with God. Our boats are tossed by God's windy Spirit, as God gets us to the place God wants us to be. As we look back from where we came, we have to admit that we were running away, but God straightened out our course.

JOURNAL: In what ways have you run away from God? What strong wind did God send to blow your ship back on course? How did you end up doing God's will?

PRAYER: Great are you, Mighty God, and worthy of all praise! Help me to know where you want me to be and what you desire that I do. Then, guide me there and enable me to do your will. Hear my prayer through Jesus Christ, the Lord. Amen.

 2

Water

With great joy,
you people will get water
from the well of victory.

—Isaiah 12:3

Separate Waters

SCRIPTURE: God said, "I command a dome to separate the water above [the earth] from the water below it." And that's what happened. God made the dome and named it "Sky." Evening came and then morning—that was the second day. God said, "I command the water under the sky to come together in one place, so there will be dry ground." And that's what happened. God named the dry ground "Land." And he named the water "Ocean." God looked at what he had done and saw that it was good (Genesis 1:6–10).

REFLECTION: As we might ask today, "From where did the sky, land, and ocean come?" so did ancient people seek an answer to the same question. We propose scientific theories, the most prominent called "the big bang." Ancient people proposed a story of origins, which we call "myth." Sometimes, we equate "myth" with non-truth or falsity. Ancient people understood myth as simply the explanation for why things are the way they are.

The first story of creation in the Hebrew Bible (Old Testament) Book of Genesis is a myth. It explains why the cosmos is the way it is. It describes the great God creating everything in six days and resting for one, which explains why there are seven days in a week, one of which is for rest. It explains why water can be found falling from the sky and contained in basins called oceans or seas—God once separated the waters with a dome and called it "sky." When the floodgates open in the dome, rain falls on the dry land. As the rain runs off the land, it flows into the container called the "ocean."

Such ancient cosmology, the way a person understands the universe in which he or she lives, and mythology, the way a person explains why he or she experiences the world as he or she does, is not our cosmology. We know that there is no dome holding back the waters above it. Rain is the result of evaporation and condensation caused by changes in temperature and wind direction. There is more than one ocean, and seas abound. Water covers two-thirds of the earth. In fact, due to travel in space, we know that the earth is not the center of our solar system, but merely another planet circling a star we have named the "sun."

Such modern cosmology and mythology do not detract from the message of the Genesis account, however. God is the creator of all that exists. Like Job, we stand in awe of the God who is manifested in the waters that fall as gentle rain and that surge as powerful waves in the oceans. "When the ocean was born," God tells Job, "I set its boundaries and wrapped it in blankets of thickest fog. Then I built a wall around it, locked the gates, and said, 'Your powerful waves stop here! They can go no farther'" (Job 38:8–11).

While Job could only answer no, we might be able to answer yes to God's questions, "Job, have you ever walked on the ocean floor?" (38:16); "Have you been to the places where I keep snow and hail . . . ? (38:22) The ocean floor and the snow and the hail still reveal God to us.

Like Job, we have to answer "God" to the questions: "Who carves out a path for the thunderstorms? Who sends torrents of rain on empty deserts where no one lives? Who is the father of the dew and of the rain? Who gives birth to the sleet and the frost that fall in winter, when streams and lakes freeze solid as a rock?" (Job 38:25–26, 28–30) And like Job, we have to answer God's "Can you?" questions with "We are not able": "Can you order the clouds to send a downpour, or will lightning flash at your command? Can you count the clouds or pour out their water on the dry, lumpy soil?" (Job 38:34–35, 37–38) All water, no matter what its form, comes from God and manifests the fluidity of God permeating all of creation with life.

JOURNAL: How do you think about or conceive the universe? Draw a picture of it. At what places do you locate water in your world? How does your understanding of the universe affect your understanding of God?

PRAYER: Creator God, you set the earth on its foundations; you gathered the waters into the oceans; you made springs gush forth in the valleys. Rain on me the grace of your Holy Spirit that I might praise you through your Son, Jesus Christ, for ever and ever. Amen.

Four Rivers

SCRIPTURE: From Eden a river flowed out to water the garden, then it divided into four rivers. The first one is the Pishon River that flows through the land of Havilah, where pure gold, rare perfumes and precious stones are found. The second is the Gihon River that winds through Ethiopia. The Tigris River that flows east of Assyria is the third, and the fourth is the Euphrates River (Genesis 2:10–14).

Reflection: God lives in the Garden of Eden, and from God, a single source, flows four rivers to the whole world. In many cultures, the number four represents totality, such as in the four corners of the earth or the four directions—north, south, east, and west. The author of the Hebrew Bible's (Old Testament's) first book, Genesis, understands that the single river coming from the garden is God, who permeates or surrounds or flows over the whole universe.

The author of the Christian Bible's last book, Revelation, also understood the single river to be God filling the world with the divine presence. The author records: "The angel showed me a river that was crystal clear, and its waters gave life. The river came from the throne where God and the Lamb were seated. Then it flowed down the middle of the city's main street. On each side of the river are trees that grow a different kind of fruit each month of the year. The fruit gives life, and the leaves are used as medicine to heal the nations" (Revelation 22:1-2).

To use a religious word, grace is the pure, crystal-clear river that flows from God and the Lamb, Jesus Christ. It is the river of the Spirit, who flows throughout the new Jerusalem, the holy city, and waters a new Garden of Eden in which life is so prolific that the trees produce twelve kinds of fruit, a different type for each month of the year. The twelve types of fruit, of course, is a direct reference to the twelve tribes of Israel and the twelve apostles. Unlike the fruit eaten in the first Garden of Eden which serves as the mythic answer for the question about from where death came, the fruit in the new Garden of Eden explains from where life and healing come for the whole world. The Lamb, who once was slain on a tree, not only reigns for ever, but has united the four divisions of the river into one life-giving torrent.

We share in this life now. It flashes forth through a painting that catches our attention and leads us into the depths of insight. The divine river emerges when we solve a crisis in our lives and know that we have reached a decision that is the right one. God fills us with enthusiasm and energy so that when we share the same with another in an intimate relationship, we realize that we are simultaneously diminished and enriched by the other, even as he or she is simultaneously diminished and enriched by us. Through our sharing, the river of grace runs deep.

Nature Spirituality

JOURNAL: In the past week, how has God's river of life flowed through your life? In what ways did you recognize God's presence in your life? How did the divine river fill you with energy and healing? What was divided and is now united?

PRAYER: Living God, you are in my midst as my refuge and strength. Grant that I may drink from your stream of grace and delight in your presence for ever. Hear my prayer in the name of Jesus Christ, the Lord. Amen.

Great Flood

SCRIPTURE: [God said to Noah and his sons:] I promise every living creature that the earth and those living on it will never again be destroyed by a flood. The rainbow that I have put in the sky will be my sign to you and to every living creature on earth. It will remind you that I will keep this promise forever. When I see the rainbow in the sky, I will always remember the promise that I have made to every living creature. (Genesis 9:11–12, 16).

REFLECTION: What do you do when things do not go exactly the way that you planned? As quickly as possible, you make alternate plans, and you try to steer things into the direction you want them to go. Through your flexibility in achieving the same end through different means, you reveal yourself as a leader. If you are not able to act fast and accomplish what you set out to do through a change in plans, you go down in defeat.

That's what the story of Noah and the great flood is all about—the ability to change plans right in the middle and still accomplish what Noah set out to do. From Noah's point of view, his plans for life were altered the day he got the message to build a huge boat and gather animals to fill it. His family, standing in the front yard and watching him assemble the floating house and barn, thought him a little crazy. But that didn't stop the patriarch from preparing for the flood. Once the rain began to fall and the rivers began to rise, all were happy to float in a dry barge. Once the washing was complete, all emerged to fill the earth with re-created goodness.

Water

From God's point of view, the plan for the earth needed retooling. Things were not going exactly the way God had wanted. From the first evil act of Adam and Eve, wickedness had flowed over the earth, continuing to infest people. So, God decided to wash clean the world and re-create the human race. Notice that the means chosen by God is water. God destroys evil with water. Sin is no superpower match for God's flowing river of goodness. Furthermore, once sin is overpowered, the earth is renewed. Noah and his family repopulate the world. The rainbow, itself water drenched with sunlight in the sky, becomes the sign of God's promise to every living creature never again to flood the earth.

However, God has not quite kept the promise. That's right; God sent another flood of God's life to wash the earth in the person of Jesus Christ. Now, through the death-defying waters of baptism, people are initiated into God's life and re-created. When we were baptized, we were flooded and drowned in the font. Then, we were raised up to newness of life. We didn't need a boat, because the great flood lasted only a few seconds. The rainbow has been replaced with the cross, representing death and life, the sign of God's promise to every living creature.

God does not fear changing plans in the middle of a project. God is always flooding the earth with God's life, washing away evil, and renewing creation. We shouldn't fear to change our plans to achieve the end for which we long. When we do, we'll most likely notice that a great flood has occurred and a rainbow spans the sky indicating the presence of the divine.

JOURNAL: When have you recently had to change your plans in the middle of something? What great flood was present? How were you washed clean? How were you renewed? What is the sign of your new plan or life?

PRAYER: Re-creating God, you set enthroned over the flood, and the waters obey your voice. May your rainbow remind me of my baptismal promises and my re-creation through your Holy Spirit in Jesus Christ, your Son, who is Lord for ever and ever. Amen.

Nature Spirituality

Water from Rock

SCRIPTURE: The [Israelites] started complaining to Moses, "Give us some water!" Then Moses prayed to the LORD, "What am I going to do with these people? They are about to stone me to death!" The LORD answered, "Take some of the leaders with you and go ahead of the rest of the people. Also take along the walking stick you used to strike the Nile River, and when you get to the rock at Mount Sinai, I will be there with you. Strike the rock with the stick, and water will pour out for the people to drink." Moses did this while the leaders watched (Exodus 17:2a, 4–6).

REFLECTION: We need water to live. In the desert, there is little water. Therefore, it is difficult to live in the desert—unless, of course, you can strike the rock and water will flow for you to drink!

We also know that if we do not get enough water, we risk dehydration. The first signs that a person is dehydrating are grumblings and complainings. If we don't get water for the individual, he or she may slip into a coma and experience kidney failure. That is how important water is to the process of sustaining life.

The Israelites were camped in the hot desert, where water evaporates fast and people can become dehydrated quickly. Their lives are at stake. They grumble because they had water from the Nile River in Egypt, where they were slaves. Now, in the desert, they have no source for water. However, what they fail to recognize in their delirium is that they thirst not only for water and life, but they thirst for God, the essence of life.

Moses gives them both. St. Paul recognized that the Israelites had all their thirsts satisfied. He told the Corinthians: "All of [the Israelites] . . . drank the same spiritual drink, which flowed from the spiritual rock that followed them. That rock was Christ" (1 Corinthians 10:3-4). Thus, when Moses struck the rock, he was tapping into the very font of God's life, which would be manifested in the person of Jesus Christ three to four thousand years later.

We are still on pilgrimage in the desert of the world, and we still thirst for the water that comes from the rock. Christ is the rock that we need only tap to get all the life-giving water we need. Today, he may be a rock of the love of a spouse who offers us the gift of himself or herself. Tap the rock and the water of life flows. Tomorrow, Christ may be the rock of a child's insight into the deep-down truth of things. Tap the child and the water of life flows for us to drink. The next day, Christ may appear as the stranger on the street, the co-worker, the student, the minister, the prisoner. Tap the rock and watch life flow for us to drink.

The Holy One satisfies our thirst for God through Christ by offering us the water of the Mighty One's own life. Yes, sometimes in our thirst we end up complaining, but God knows that we are thirsty. Drinking deeply of the water that flows from the rock of Christ, who is God, means that we thirst for more and more and more. God's stream is unlimited.

JOURNAL: What rock have you recently tapped and drank from? Of what kind of life did you drink? Was your thirst preceded by any grumbling or complaining? How is God manifested in your source of life-giving water?

PRAYER: God my Rock, I long for you like a deer longs for flowing streams. I thirst for you, the living God. Give me to drink of your Holy Spirit through your Son, Jesus Christ. All praise be yours now and for ever. Amen.

Crossing the Jordan

SCRIPTURE: The priests carrying the chest walked in front, until they came to the Jordan River. The water in the river had risen over its banks, as it often does in springtime. But as soon as the feet of the priests touched the water, the river stopped flowing, and the water started piling up. . . . No water flowed toward the Dead Sea, and the priests stood in the middle of the dry riverbed . . . while everyone else crossed over (Joshua 3:14–17).

REFLECTION: The narrative of the crossing of the Jordan River in the Hebrew Bible (Old Testament) Book of Joshua is a miniature version of Moses' leading the Israelites dry-shod through the Sea of Reeds. Just as Moses led the people from Egyptian slavery to freedom, Joshua, Moses' successor, leads the people from the desert into the land flowing with milk and honey. A new "Exodus" is needed. And, of course, it involves water.

The chest carried by the priests, sometimes called the "ark of the covenant," contains the tablets of the law, Moses' staff, and a jar of manna. Upon the top of the chest two creatures, called cherubim, spread their wings and form a throne for God. Thus, the chest is a sign of God's presence with Israel. No wonder the water stops flowing when the feet of the priests carrying the chest step into the Jordan River! Just as God parted the Sea of Reeds, so God parts the Jordan River. The crossings represent leaving one lifestyle behind and walking into a new way of living.

All of us cross rivers. The crossing may not contain the drama of Joshua's exodus through the Jordan River, but upon examination we see that something was crossed and new life was found. Maybe it was solving a moral dilemma. We thought and read and agonized over the right thing to do, finally made the decisive crossing, and lived with our decision. The river could have consisted of a change in careers. After twenty years of doing the same job, we decided to go back to school, learn a new river-crossing skill, and get a new job. When people decide to become parents through birth or adoption, they cross the river of responsibility to care for another, and that certainly changes the way they live.

God leads us through the river and on the opposite bank offers us new life. Ask Moses and Joshua and the Israelites, and they will tell you how God helped them cross rivers.

Journal: What major rivers have you crossed in your life? How did God lead you to the river? How did God help you cross? What new life did you find on the opposite bank?

Prayer: Almighty God, once you turned the Sea of Reeds into dry land so your people could pass through. At the Jordan you parted the waters so that the Israelites could find new life in the promised land. Throughout my life, make my river crossings safe and lead me to your reign with Jesus Christ, your Son, and the Holy Spirit, one God for ever and ever. Amen.

Rain Stopped

Scripture: Elijah was a prophet from Tishbe in Gilead. One day he went to King Ahab and said, "I'm a servant of the living LORD, the God of

Water

Israel. And I swear in his name that it won't rain until I say so. There won't even be any dew on the ground." Later, the LORD said to Elijah, "Leave and go across the Jordan River so you can hide near Cherith Creek. You can drink water from the creek, and eat the food I've told the ravens to bring you." Elijah obeyed the LORD and went to live near Cherith Creek. Ravens brought him bread and meat twice a day, and he drank water from the creek. But after a while, it dried up because there was no rain (1 Kings 17:1–5).

REFLECTION: Notice the use of water in the five verses of the story about Elijah above. There is water in the form of rain and dew. There is water in the creek to drink. No matter what form it takes, water is everywhere. And it is a fitting metaphor to describe God, who is everywhere.

The Holy One is removing God's presence from the land of Israel. The metaphor is that it will not rain again until Elijah, God's prophet, says it will. God is vacating Israel because of King Ahab's wickedness. "Ahab did more things to disobey the LORD than any king before him" (1 Kings 16:30), states the author of the Hebrew Bible's (Old Testament's) First Book of Kings. The state of the king and the people, who follow his lead, will be reflected in the land, which will turn barren because of no rain. The people are so dry that not even dew will appear on the grass.

Elijah crosses the Jordan River, a boundary. On the other side of the Jordan there is water to drink and food to eat, provided by the hand of God. God is present, ironically, not where God is presumed to be—with the king of Israel—but with Elijah on the other side of the river, near a flowing creek, where ravens deliver a daily portion of bread and meat. God is with Elijah.

With no rain, however, even Cherith Creek dries up. But God does not abandon the prophet, who is instructed to go to Zarephath in Sidon, further away from Israel, where there is a very powerless widow and her son. Not only does she have no man to care for her, but she has only a handful of flour and a little olive oil. What happens when God enters her home? Elijah proclaims that her flour won't run out and her bottle of oil won't dry up before it rains again. Notice that God is once again exactly where God is not supposed to be—with a foreigner.

A lack of faith, a lack of trust, makes people dry up. They are like the land without rain. Without God people are as dry as a creek in the desert in the middle of the summer. With God, people are like the trees along the river that flourish. Elijah believes in God even when his king does not.

Nature Spirituality

Elijah trusts God even when Ahab does not. The widow believes in and trusts God's word delivered by Elijah. Those who believe and trust discover the rain falling all around them. Those who do not believe and trust dry up, because not even dew forms on the grass around them.

Journal: How have you experienced yourself as being without rain? To what creek did God lead you? What rain fell upon you? What widow met your needs? How is God like water all around you?

Prayer: All-powerful God, you cannot be limited in your care for those who trust your promises. Make me like a tree planted by a stream of water that I may yield fruit and never wither. I make this prayer in the name of Jesus Christ, who is Lord for ever and ever. Amen.

Water and Fire

Scripture: Elijah dug a ditch around the altar, large enough to hold about thirteen quarts. He placed the wood on the altar, then they cut the bull into pieces and laid the meat on the wood.

He told the people, "Fill four large jars with water and pour it over the meat and the wood." After they did this, he told them to do it two more times. They did exactly as he said until finally, the water ran down the altar and filled the ditch.

When it was time for the evening sacrifice, Elijah prayed. . . . The LORD immediately sent fire, and it burned up the sacrifice, the wood, and the stones. It scorched the ground everywhere around the altar and dried up every drop of water in the ditch. When the crowd saw what had happened, they all bowed down and shouted, "The LORD is God! The LORD is God!" (1 Kings 18:32–36, 38–39)

Reflection: Elijah makes it as difficult as possible for the Holy One to demonstrate God's power to the people. Of course, God is already present—in contrast to the foreign deity Baal, whose prophets cannot get him to answer their prayers and to accept the sacrificial bull which they have prepared.

Elijah signifies God's presence by using twelve stones to build the altar. The stones, of course, represent the twelve tribes of Israel, Jacob's twelve sons, the incarnate sign of God fulfilling the promise made to Abraham, Jacob's father, that his descendants would be as countless as the stars in the sky or the sand on the sea shore.

The prophet also demonstrates that God is present on Mount Carmel—notice that all this takes place on the top of a mountain, where not only the pagan gods lived but where God was supposed to live. Taking four jars of water—four signifying the four directions of the world—and filling them three times each—indicating a theophany, a manifestation of God, and totaling twelve—the number of Jacob's sons, Elijah prays that God will accept the sacrificial bull—reminiscent of the covenant between God and Israel sealed in the blood of bulls sprinkled on the people by Moses at Mount Sinai.

Elijah knew all along that God was already present through the sign of water. Now the Holy One uses the ancient sign of fire not only to burn up the watery sacrifice, the wood, and the altar, but to scorch the land and dry it up. The lack of wetness after having poured out so much water indicates the state of the faith of the people who have strayed from their God to the worship of Baal.

The impossibility of fire drying up water (water usually puts out fire) is possible from God's point of view. Elijah believed that. Elijah knew that God is always present and demonstrates it through water and fire.

Journal: In what ways have you recognized God's presence in your life through the signs of water and fire? What sacrifice were you offering? In what ways had you strayed from God or began to doubt? What was the impossible that became possible?

Prayer: Mighty God, you summon the earth from the rising of the sun to its setting. You reveal your presence in water and fire. Keep me faithful to your ways and ever alert to your presence in my life. Hear my prayer through Jesus Christ, who is Lord for ever and ever. Amen.

Divided Water

SCRIPTURE: Elijah and Elisha were walking along [the Jordan River] and talking, when suddenly there appeared between them a flaming chariot pulled by fiery horses. Right away, a strong wind took Elijah up into heaven. Elijah's coat had fallen off, so Elisha picked it up and walked back to the Jordan River. He struck the water with the coat and wondered, "Will the LORD perform miracles for me as he did for Elijah?" As soon as Elisha did this, a dry path opened up through the water, and he walked across (2 Kings 2:11, 13–14).

REFLECTION: The Hebrew Bible (Old Testament) cycle of stories featuring Elijah and his successor, Elisha, as prophets of Israel is viewed through the lens of the tales about Moses, Israel's law-giver, and his successor, Joshua. Just as "Moses stretched his arm over the sea, and the LORD sent a strong east wind that blew all night until there was dry land where the water had been" (Exodus 14:21), and just as Joshua instructed the priests carrying the chest containing the tablets of the law to step into the Jordan River and "the river stopped flowing . . . and the priests stood in the middle of the dry riverbed near Jericho while everyone else crossed over" (Joshua 3:16-17), so does Elijah strike the river with his coat in order to part the waters and is followed in this action by Elisha.

Dividing the water is a sign of changing boundaries, of leaving one way of life and beginning another. Moses led the people from a life of slavery to one of freedom. Joshua led them out of their fear of their enemies across the border as conquerors and founders of a new land flowing with milk and honey. Elijah crossed the boundary of this world into the fiery world of God. Elisha became Elijah's successor and divided the Jordan River in order to deliver the word of the Holy One to God's people.

In modern thought, dividing the water is an experience of conversion, the leaving of one way of life and the embracing of another way of life. Christians celebrate that breaking of boundaries with baptism. A person is plunged into the dividing waters to cross over and never to be exactly the same again. At the time of death, water is sprinkled over the deceased to indicate that he or she has crossed another boundary, the one dividing this visible world from the invisible one.

Indeed, we spend most of our lives dividing water, crossing boundaries, being changed, converted. Such water-dividing experiences may involve marriage, the rearing of children, being retrained for a new job, embracing a new career, retirement. Of whatever it consists, we can be sure that a sea or a river was crossed.

Journal: What water have you most recently divided? What did you leave behind and with what did you move forward? What was the sign of God's presence with you as you crossed over (such as a staff and wind for Moses, the chest for Joshua, the fiery chariot for Elijah, and Elisha's coat for Elisha)?

Prayer: Eternal God, you led your prophets throughout their lives as you converted them over and over again to your ways. Lead me during my lifetime pilgrimage. I thank you for your steadfast love and all your wonderful works through Jesus Christ, your Son, who is Lord for ever and ever. Amen.

Washed Clean

Scripture: Naaman was the commander of the Syrian army. Naaman was a brave soldier, but he had leprosy. Elisha sent someone . . . to say to him, "Go wash seven times in the Jordan River. Then you'll be completely cured." Naaman walked down to the Jordan; he waded out into the water and stooped down in it seven times, just as Elisha had told him. Right away, he was cured, and his skin became as smooth as a child's. Naaman and his officials went back to Elisha. Naaman stood in front of him and announced, "Now I know that the God of Israel is the only God in the whole world" (2 Kings 1ac, 10, 14–15b).

Reflection: Ouray, Colorado, a mountain town, is well known for its hot springs, which are channeled to several motel/hotel pools and one large public swimming pool. The public facility is divided into several sections ranging from the hottest to the coolest water. Heated by the earth's core before it comes flowing out of the mountains, the water is known for its healing properties. It relieves the aches and pains of arthritis and rheumatism, and it can be very soothing after spending a few hours on the ski slopes.

Nature Spirituality

The warm waters of Ouray do not compare to the muddy Jordan River in the ancient world. At first, Naaman is reluctant to go and dip himself into those murky waters, especially when there are clear streams in his homeland of Syria. But after a little urging, the non-Israelite follows the prophet Elisha's simple message to wash seven times in order to be cured.

What Elisha knows is that it is not the water that cures Naaman; God does the curing. Signified by the number seven, representing completeness, God, who is perfect, makes Naaman whole. And more astoundingly, Naaman recognizes that Israel's God is the only One in the whole world. That's quite a statement for a pagan army commander! It becomes even more shocking in the context of Israel's wondering away from God and the people's embracing of the foreign gods of their neighboring nations.

Literally, we are washed into wholeness on a daily basis. Our morning shower cleanses us of the previous day's grime and the sleep of last night. We emerge from the warm bath renewed and ready to face another day. Maybe a portion of our day will be spent in a health or fitness center which may have a sauna—a type of water bath, a steam room—another type of water bath, a hot tub, or a Jacuzzi. After a workout, the heat and water bring healing to stretched muscles.

When healing takes place, no matter what the source of the water, our faith is also revived in the God of Israel. Our God is interested in the wholeness of Israelites and pagans alike. Our God is interested in the wholeness of all people.

Journal: In what ways has water healed you? Characterize the wholeness that resulted. How did the healing you experienced also strengthen your faith? Were there any significant signs accompanying your healing that pointed toward God?

Prayer: Healing God, you cure disease and renew people with life. Wash me into your wholeness as I profess my faith in you, Father, Son, and Holy Spirit, one God for ever and ever. Amen.

Snow and Ice

Scripture: By [the Holy One's] command he sends the driving snow. . . . He scatters the snow like birds flying down, and its descent is like locusts alighting. The eye is dazzled by the beauty of its whiteness, and the mind is amazed as it falls. He pours frost over the earth like salt, and icicles form like pointed thorns. The cold north wind blows, and ice freezes on the water; it settles on every pool of water, and the water puts it on like a breastplate (Sirach 43:13a, 17c–20).

REFLECTION: The author of the Hebrew Bible (Old Testament) Book of Sirach, sometimes called Ecclesiasticus, writes several chapters about the works of God in nature. By reflecting on snow and ice, for example, Jesus son of Sirach—the traditional name of the author of the book—declares that God can be "seen" in creation.

God sends the driving snow to the earth. Notice that the snow is like birds flying from the sky to the land and like a swarm of locusts descending upon a field. The whiteness of the snow blinds the eye and seduces the mind into reflecting upon it. We often speak about the uniqueness of every snowflake and how no two are exactly the same. That thought can launch a person into a meditation upon the uniqueness of the millions of people who populate the earth and, yet, no two are exactly alike. We can compare falling snow to feathers floating on the wind to the earth. After a snowfall and the sun begins to shine, we put on sunglasses to protect our eyes from the brightness, to hide ourselves from the presence of the Holy One.

In the deep freeze of winter, blasts of cold from the Arctic descend upon us. The north wind cuts right through us, chilling us to the bone. The wind-chill is more dangerous than the actual temperature. On windshields and windows the north wind sketches abstract designs in frost, which can help us marvel at the unlimited possibilities of the Creator as we scrape it away. Farm ponds and lakes protect the life within them by donning breastplates of ice upon which we skate and wonder how we can actually walk on water.

As the snow and ice melt, icicles form on the edges of the roofs of buildings. Each thorn-like stalactite differs from the members of its family as they grow together and, finally, drips to a dry death. Barren tree branches cradle the ice and snow, while evergreens bend with their burden in worship of God.

The Holy One leaves God's mark everywhere. Snow and ice, frost and icicles offer us the opportunity to appreciate the Master Artist at work during the winter.

Nature Spirituality

JOURNAL: After recalling the last time you watched the snow fall, make a list of the metaphors you might use to describe it (such as "like birds flying down"). Do the same for ice, frost, and icicles. How does each reveal God to you?

PRAYER: Praise to you, God. You send snow like wool, scatter frost like ashes, and hurl hail like crumbs. Then, you send the sun to melt them and make the waters flow. Make me grateful for all your gifts through Jesus Christ, who is Lord for ever and ever. Amen.

Well of Victory

SCRIPTURE: With great joy, you people will get water from the well of victory. At that time you will say, "Our LORD, we are thankful, and we worship only you. We will tell the nations how glorious you are and what you have done. Because of your wonderful deeds we will sing your praises everywhere on earth" (Isaiah 12:3–5).

REFLECTION: The book of the prophet Isaiah, whom most biblical scholars believe was written by three different authors, uses water consistently throughout his sixty-six chapters. Above, the prophet declares that the Israelites will draw water from a well of victory. The victory would consist of their release from Babylonian captivity and their return to Jerusalem. In a song of praise, Isaiah declares that God will bring them back to their own land, where they will praise the Mighty One for God's deeds.

In another section of the book, the prophet focuses on what the Holy one does for God's people. In this case, it is the poor. The prophet records: "When the poor and needy are dying of thirst and cannot find water, I, the LORD God of Israel, will come to their rescue. I won't forget them. I will make rivers flow on mountain peaks. I will send streams to fill the valleys. Dry and barren land will flow with springs and become a lake" (41:17–18). Thus, the poor and needy will be cared for by God.

Both the land and people are taken care of by the Creator. In words similar to those above, the prophet portrays God as saying: "I will bless the thirsty land by sending streams of water: I will bless your descendants by giving them my Spirit. They will spring up like grass or like willow trees near flowing streams" (44:3–4).

On their way from captivity to freedom, the Israelites will not go hungry or get thirsty. God will be merciful while leading them along to streams of water (cf. 49:10). Then, in what may be the most beautiful invitation in the Hebrew Bible (Old Testament), Isaiah records God as saying: "I, the LORD, promise to bless you with victory. If you are thirsty, come and drink water!" (55:1ab). God promises to bring people to the new Jerusalem. They will be victorious over their enemies and drink from the well of God.

The prophet uses water so much because it was a precious commodity to a people who lived a long time in the desert. The images of drinking from the well and streams is not only a metaphor for God's care, but is another way of saying that people drink of God. That is why God says that the people's descendants will be blessed through God's gift of the Spirit. When they drink from the well or from the streams, they drink of God, the source of life. The Holy One gave us Jesus, whom the author of John's Gospel records as saying: "If you are thirsty, come to me and drink! Have faith in me, and you will have life-giving water flowing from deep inside you . . ." (7:37b–38). He drank from the well of victory. Raised from the dead, he became the river of eternal life from which we drink.

JOURNAL: For what do you thirst? For whom do you thirst? In what ways has God satisfied your thirst? In what ways does God satisfy the earth's thirst? What is the well of victory from which you drink?

PRAYER: Mighty God, streams of grace flow from you to your people to drink. Give me the life-giving water of Jesus Christ that I may drink abundantly from him who is Lord for ever and ever. Amen.

Rejected Water

SCRIPTURE: The LORD told me [, Jeremiah,] to go to Jerusalem and tell everyone that he had said: I am the true and glorious God, but you have rejected me to worship idols. You, my people, have sinned in two ways—you have rejected me, the source of life-giving water, and you've tried to collect water in cracked and leaking pits dug in the ground (Jeremiah 2:1–2a, 11b, 13).

Nature Spirituality

REFLECTION: In the book of the prophet Jeremiah, water signifies God, whom the Israelites have rejected in order to worship idols. Because they no longer remember their origins, the Israelites are like cracked cisterns which will not hold water. God wants to pour God's life into them, but they are like a colander and it runs right through them, says Jeremiah. Until they give up their idol-worship, they are not able to be filled with God's life.

Forgetting is a human characteristic. We forget to put out the garbage for pickup. We forget to turn off the lights in our car and run down the battery. Failing to keep a promise made to another is forgetting. When the Israelites forgot their Creator, the God who had called Abraham and Sarah, the God who had led the twelve tribes of Israel out of Egypt, the God who had subdued enemies, they turned to the gods of their neighboring nations and worshiped them. They forgot their source of life and went looking for it in contaminated wells.

Jeremiah declares that the people resemble what they have become. They are cracked and leaking, unable to be filled with life-giving water. By remembering the glory God once shared with them, they can repent and return to the source of their life. Through conversion, Israel will be healed and filled with life-giving water.

Often, we turn from God to the idols of our time and begin to leak. We don't worship gods made of wood or brass; our idols are much more subtle. "The right look" can become god for us. Think of how many people subscribe to the theory that the clothes make the man or woman. If clothes haven't become idols, then why do lawyers, bankers, and accountants all look alike? Why do teens kill each other in order to take each other's clothes and shoes?

"The right look" also includes the perfect body. Men and women spend hours lifting weights in order to present well-sculpted muscles. Add the right degree of tan and the creature becomes the idol. If this were not true, why do people spend so much time working out in gyms? Or why must children be deterred from imitating such behavior?

"The right look" includes beards, mustaches, goatees, the right color of hair and plenty of it for men. For women, the right foundation, color of lipstick and eye shadow, and hair color form a beautiful face. If we look good, we feel good, the proverb says, but we also can become the idol we worship.

Clothes are important, as is health and personal appearance, but when we forget who God is, we can become like the Israelites and worship our own handmade idols. Our source of life-giving water, God, is forgotten, and our healthy, well-clad, good-looking bodies are really leaking pits. As quickly as God is filling us with life, it is running out through the cracks in us.

Journal: What do you think are the idols of our society? Make a list and explain how you think each is an idol. What are your personal idols? Make a list and explain how each makes you a cracked cistern leaking the life God offers you. What do you need to do to repair your well so that God can fill you with life.

Prayer: Merciful God, when your people forgot you and turned to idols, you called them back to the source of life-giving water. Make me aware of my personal gods that I may not turn to them in times of trial but trust you, who graciously redeem me through Jesus Christ the Lord. Amen.

Clean Water

Scripture: [God told Ezekiel to tell the Israelites:] I will sprinkle you with clean water, and you will be clean and acceptable to me. I will wash away everything that makes you unclean, and I will remove your disgusting idols. You will once again live in the land I gave your ancestors; you will be my people, and I will be your God (Ezekiel 36:25, 28).

Reflection: One quality of water is its ability to purify, to depollute. We use water to cleanse a wound or a scrape. Before entering the operating room, doctors scrub their hands and arms to remove anything that might infect their patients. Dishes and eating utensils are purified by washing them with soap and water in the kitchen sink or by placing them in the dishwasher.

God tells the priestly prophet Ezekiel to proclaim to the Israelites that the Holy One will purify them. They were not dirty in terms of needing to be physically washed; their pollution came from their idol-worship. They had fallen away from God, but God would bring them back.

Their purification would include the removal of their stubbornness, here understood to be their lack of conversion. How often do we need to have our stubborn hearts cleansed? Particularly when we are confronted by someone, we tend to dig in our heels and not budge an inch. Our "being right" can be like blinders on either side of our heads, blocking our peripheral view and prohibiting us from seeing the big picture. In Ezekiel's time, the city of Jerusalem had fallen to the enemy and the people had been taken away in captivity, but still they worshiped idols. They might listen to the prophet's words, but they did not change. God promises to purify such blindness.

The gift of God's Spirit is also promised to the people. The Spirit, the sharing of God's own self with people, will plant the seed of faithfulness in their hearts and minds. Their thoughts will be pure, and they will want to obey God's laws and teachings. God's cleansing water will touch the whole person. The bath will not be a mere washing away of dirt, but, rather, an inner scrubbing of that which motivates action. Deep inside is where change occurs and roots and, finally, blossoms on the outside.

God's clean water sprinkled upon God's people will enable them to return to their own country. But more so, God will claim the Israelites as his people again. The Holy One will be their God, and they will be God's people. Once God washes us clean, the Holy One claims us. Through the waters of baptism, we are purified, oriented toward God, and, simultaneously, claimed by God. We are even promised further cleansing when we need it.

What Ezekiel recognized is that God is the clean water. The Mighty One sprinkles God's self on people. Some people call this action grace. Whatever name we give, it is the all-powerful God who purifies us, makes us clean, and places a new heart and the Holy One's own Spirit within us.

JOURNAL: From what stubbornness has God cleansed you? What pure thoughts has God placed within you? In what ways has God poured the Spirit into you? Where is God leading you?

PRAYER: Creator God, the earth is yours as is all that is in it. Give me clean hands and a pure heart that I may approach you blamelessly. Send your Holy Spirit to live with me as I strive to follow Jesus Christ, your Son, who is Lord for ever and ever. Amen.

Temple Water

SCRIPTURE: The man took me [, Ezekiel,] back to the temple, where I saw a stream flowing from under the entrance. It began in the south part of the temple, where it ran past the altar and continued east through the courtyard. We walked out of the temple area through the north gate and went around to the east gate. I saw the small stream of water flowing east from the south side of the gate. The man said: This water flows eastward.... Wherever this water flows, there will be all kinds of animals and fish, because it will bring life and fresh water.... Fruit trees will grow all along this river and produce fresh fruit every month (Ezekiel 47:1–2, 8a, 9, 12a).

REFLECTION: In the prophet Ezekiel's vision, the temple, one of the places where God was localized on earth, is the source of all life. While the vision may look like one day from the first story of creation in the Book of Genesis, it portrays God as being the origin of water and life. From under the entrance to the temple God's life flows. What begins as a small stream turns into a deep river spreading life to animals, fish, and trees. Using a contemporary hospital metaphor, God is a single intravenous unit to which everything is connected.

The author of the Christian Bible (New Testament) Book of Revelation both employed and transformed Ezekiel's vision. In the new Jerusalem, the author says: "I did not see a temple.... The Lord God All-Powerful and the Lamb were its temple" (21:22). The visionary also sees "a river that was crystal clear, and its waters gave life. The river came from the throne where God and the Lamb were seated. Then it flowed down the middle of the city's main street. On each side of the river are trees that grow a different kind of fruit each month of the year. The fruit gives life... (22:1–2).

The message of the author of Revelation is the same as Ezekiel: God is the source of all life. The water, flowing from God, is a metaphor for God's life which the Holy One offers to people. All we need to do is to drink deeply of it and eat the fruit of the trees which further enhances life and heals it.

No matter where we imagine God's temple or throne to be, water flows from it. Some people think of God's residence as being in the sky, from which the rain falls and causes the earth to bear fruit. Some of us may think that God lives in our churches, where we have our hearts and

Nature Spirituality

minds refreshed with the word of God, the sacraments of Christ, and the inspiration of the Spirit. Other people make think of God's home as being their own body, a temple of Spirit. God works in and through them, making them bear fruit which serves to give life to others.

Unlike a single small stream in nature, which, unless it is joined by more branches, quickly disappears by being absorbed by the earth, God's stream keeps getting deeper and deeper. There is an abundance of God's water, enough for everyone and everything to drink and to have life.

JOURNAL: Where do you locate God's temple, throne, or house? What water flows from it? In what ways have you drunk from God's stream? What fruit have your borne? What fruit have others borne and shared with you?

PRAYER: Life-living God, your throne is in heaven, but you share your grace with all you have created. May I drink deeply of your Spirit and come to share the eternal life of Jesus Christ, your Son, who is Lord for ever and ever. Amen.

Split Water

SCRIPTURE: [John the Baptist told the people:] "Someone more powerful is going to come. I baptize you with water, but he will baptize you with the Holy Spirit!" About that time Jesus came from Nazareth in Galilee, and John baptized him in the Jordan River. As soon as Jesus came out of the water, he saw the sky open and the Holy Spirit coming down to him like a dove. A voice from heaven said, "You are my own dear Son, and I am pleased with you" (Mark 1:7a, 8–11).

REFLECTION: Most biblical scholars accept Mark's Gospel as the oldest account of the Good News in the Christian Bible (New Testament), written around 70 CE. Thus, while there are parallel stories of Jesus' baptism in Matthew (3:13–17) and Luke (3:21–22), both authors have adapted Mark's account to serve their own purposes and illustrate themes in their gospels.

Water

When we read Mark's account of Jesus' baptism, several signs guide us on our way. First, there is no doubt that John baptized Jesus, a fact which will raise a question about who is greater (John or Jesus?) by the time Matthew and Luke begin to write (80-90 CE) and which will influence their adaptations of the story.

Second, John says that the Jesus he baptizes will in turn baptize—not with water but with the Holy Spirit, God. In Mark's account, Jesus becomes the Messiah, the Anointed One, when the Holy Spirit comes upon him, like Samuel pouring oil over David's head. "At that moment, the Spirit of the LORD took control of David and stayed with him from then on" (1 Samuel 16:13). The Holy Spirit names Jesus as the Christ, the Anointed One.

Third, the focus of attention in the story is not the dove, another image of the Holy Spirit, but the opened sky. In a three-storied universe, God lived above the dome that held back the waters above and covered the plate-like earth. People lived on the flat surface of the world, and the dead lived below in a cave-like place called Sheol. If the sky is opened or ripped apart, the waters above the dome flood the earth. Even more, God falls onto the earth—simultaneously a joyous and a terrifying thought.

It is joyous to think of God being with people wherever they are. But the people of the ancient world had located God in the meeting tent Moses had built and in several shrines until the Temple was built in Jerusalem by David's son, Solomon. In the Holy of Holies God lived on earth, like God lived above the dome of the sky in Hebrew cosmology. What the author of Mark's Gospel proclaims as Good News is that God has come to live on earth in the person of Jesus. In fact, as Mark narrates later in his story, immediately upon Jesus death, "the curtain in the temple tore in two from top to bottom" (15:38). Thus, God escaped and was roaming around the earth with people!

Like the Israelites of old who walked through the parted sea, Jesus parted the water of the Jordan River when he was baptized in it. He not only parted the water on the earth, he split open the waters above the dome, indeed, the entire universe, to declare that God is exactly where people would not have looked—with them. God anointed not only Jesus with the Holy Spirit, but true to John the Baptist's prediction, the Holy One anointed the whole world with Spirit, God's presence. We are bathed in Spirit.

JOURNAL: In what ways have you been anointed with the Holy Spirit? What was split open as a result? What were the signs that God was living with you? How were you both joyous and afraid?

Prayer: Creator God, give me a clean heart and put a new and right spirit within me. Enable me to follow Jesus more closely and drink more deeply of the Holy Spirit. I give you praise now and for ever. Amen.

Water into Wine

Scripture: . . . Mary, the mother of Jesus, was at a wedding feast in the village of Cana in Galilee. Jesus and his disciples had also been invited and were there. When the wine was all gone, Mary said to Jesus, "They don't have any more wine." Jesus told the servants to fill [the six stone water jars, each holding about twenty or thirty gallons] to the top with water. Then . . . he said, "Now take some water and give it to the man in charge of the feast." . . . The man in charge drank some of the water that had now turned into wine. He called the bridegroom over and said, "The best wine is always served first. But you have kept the best until last!" (John 2:1–3, 7–8a, 9a, 9c–10ac)

Reflection: This account of the water turned into wine is found only in John's Gospel in which the narrator of the story declares it to be Jesus' first of seven signs. The question it poses to the reader is: Of what is it a sign?

As is the case for most signs in John's Gospel, the answer is plural. Signs in the Fourth Gospel are polyvalent, meaning that each has many references pointing toward the presence of God. In other words, while the story is perfectly understandable on one level of discourse, it can refer to other things when viewed from another angle.

For example, the mother of Jesus is a sign of the church. In John's Gospel she makes only two appearances: One is at the wedding feast and the other at the foot of the cross, where she is entrusted to the care of the beloved disciple and he is given to her as a son. From this understanding, Christians refer to Mary as Mother of the Church.

Another sign is the wedding feast. The union of God with people throughout the Hebrew Bible (Old Testament) is signified by a marriage covenant celebrated with a great dinner, fine foods, and choice wines. The prophet Isaiah uses that image for the return of the Jews to Jerusalem after the Babylonian exile. The entire book of the prophet Hosea is focused on the breaking and reuniting of the two parties, God and people, bound by their wedding vows.

The water turned into wine is a double sign. Water, used in John's Gospel to signify new birth, God's life, eternal life, the Holy Spirit, and more, flows from the side of Jesus after he dies on the cross. Like Adam from whose side God took a rib and created a woman, from the side of Jesus a new people is created. Water baptizes them into the church and fills them with infinite, divine life. The wine references eucharist, the drinking of Christ's blood. In John's Gospel there is no eucharistic institution narrative, but in chapter six there is a lengthy monologue, part of which focuses on the importance of drinking Christ's blood, called true drink, in order to be one with him and to have eternal life. Thus, after Jesus' death on the cross, he gives birth to baptism (water) and eucharist (blood, wine), adding still another referent to the signs of water and wine presented at the wedding feast.

All of these signs indicate the divine presence. When we feast, God is there with us. When we eat and drink in memory of Jesus, we can be assured that God is filling us with eternal life. Christ is the bridegroom, and we are the bride. He has entered into a marriage covenant with us and sealed it with water and wine.

Journal: What are the signs of your marriage covenant with Christ? Make a list of what water and wine can signify for you. How does each signification help to make you aware of God's presence?

Prayer: God of the covenant, you bring forth food from the earth to fill your creatures and wine to gladden their hearts. Through the water and blood of your Son, Jesus Christ, you have joined all people to yourself in order to share your own life. Bring me to the eternal marriage feast where Jesus is Lord for ever and ever. Amen.

Water and Spirit

Scripture: Jesus replied [to Nicodemus], "I tell you for certain that you must be born from above before you can see God's kingdom!" Nicodemus asked, "How can a grown man ever be born a second time?" Jesus replied: . . . You must be born not only by water, but by the

Spirit. Only God's Spirit gives new life. The Spirit is like the wind that blows wherever it wants to. You can hear the wind, but you don't know where it comes from or where it is going" (John 3:3–5, 8).

Reflection: The man named Nicodemus is unique to John's Gospel in which he makes three appearances: a visit to Jesus during the night (above), a defense of Jesus before the Pharisees and chief priests (7:50–51), and the burial of Jesus (19:39). As are the other characters in John's Gospel, Nicodemus is a sign representing how a person comes to faith. He begins by coming to Jesus in the dark of night, then he defends him before his fellow Pharisees, and, finally, he helps to bury him. Through these three scenes in the gospel, the author shows us how Nicodemus is born of water and the Spirit.

The emphasis of the dialogue between Jesus and Nicodemus is placed on being born from above of water and Spirit. The wise leader must be taught by the untrained Jesus. At first, Nicodemus thinks that Jesus is talking about crawling back into his mother's womb and being born a second time. Jesus is talking about reflecting on life experiences and discovering the pattern of death and rebirth that is etched across human existence. It begins with the breaking of water preceding birth, the announcement that a mother's child is about to leave the womb, and culminates in being born, entering the world for the first time.

Christianity views baptism as a second birth. St. Augustine called the baptismal font "the womb of the church" from which many children were given new birth. The church is our mother. Like the water of the child's mother broke before birth, so the waters of the font are broken by the invocation of the Spirit upon the water before the child or adult is immersed into it. The prayer for the Spirit is further dramatized by the minister laying hands on the water. During the Easter Vigil, the Easter candle, the sign of the risen Christ, is plunged into the water to make it fruitful and to fill it with the Spirit of Christ.

The Spirit, signified by water, touches the spirit of the person as it envelopes him or and her and fills the individual with divine life. The one who dies in the water, signified by immersion, rises renewed, washed, and made fruitful by the Spirit of God. This beginning of the dying and rising process continues throughout one's life. Every time we willingly die to self, possessions, desires, we discover an abundance of water and Spirit flowing through our lives.

JOURNAL: When have you most recently experienced being born again? What dying did you do? What new life did you discover? How was God present to you (as water, wind, word)? How has your faith been enhanced?

PRAYER: Creator God, you knit me together in my mother's womb and filled me with life. Through water and Spirit, you gave me a rebirth and filled me with eternal life. Keep me faithful to the promises I made in baptism and lead me to your domain, where Jesus is Lord for ever and ever. Amen.

Living Water

SCRIPTURE: . . . A Samaritan woman came to draw water from the well. Jesus asked her, "Would you please give me a drink of water?" She replied, "How can you ask me for a drink of water when Jews and Samaritans won't have anything to do with each other?" Jesus answered, "You don't know what God wants to give you, and you don't know who is asking you for a drink. If you did, you would ask me for the water that gives life." "Sir," the woman said, "you don't even have a bucket, and the well is deep. Where are you going to get this life-giving water?" Jesus answered, "Everyone who drinks this water will get thirsty again. But no one who drinks the water I give will ever be thirsty again. The water I give is like a flowing fountain that gives eternal life" (John 4:7–8, 9b–11, 13–14).

REFLECTION: Sometimes when a person is telling a joke, he or she employs a figure of speech we call a double entendre, a word or phrase which can have two or more connotations depending upon how the hearer understands it. John's Gospel is full of double entendres, such as water in the story about Jesus and the Samaritan woman. As we read the story, we are confronted with two meanings of water—water in the well and life-giving water flowing from within a person.

The narrative begins with the Johannine Jesus sitting beside Jacob's well and requesting a drink from a Samaritan woman. In the culture of the time, not only should Jesus not have been initiating a conversation with a woman, but he should not have even looked at her since she was a Samaritan, a social outcast. Cultural boundaries, however, never stop Jesus. He ignores the double taboo (Samaritan woman) and proceeds to engage her in conversation.

At first she understands him to be asking for a drink of physical water, like that in the well. Suddenly, however, well-water becomes living water, the life of God. The woman, who can come to the well to get her daily portion of water, is told by Jesus to ask for life-giving water. If she professes her faith in Jesus as the Son of God, she will be like a fountain gushing eternal life.

Gradually, the Samaritan woman catches on to what Jesus means by water. She professes her faith, leaves her bucket at the well, and goes to evangelize others. She, who at the beginning of the story was an outcast, becomes a proclaimer of the gospel at the end of the story. She gushes with the water of eternal life, God's life. In the person of Jesus, she has discovered the God who desires to satisfy her thirst.

We, too, thirst for God. At first we may think that we need only a glass of water from the kitchen sink, but quickly we discover that we are thirsty again and again. Faith is not something we give to ourselves. Faith is a gift that God gives to us to satisfy our thirst. God moves toward us and tells us to drink from the well that will satisfy our thirst for ever. When we do, we begin to overflow with the divine life that needs no bucket but which can quench our thirst eternally. And others can drink from us as God works through us, as God did through the Samaritan woman, to flood the world with God's eternal life.

JOURNAL: For what do you thirst? Make a list. What will satisfy each thirst? For what do you thirst spiritually? Make a list. What life-giving water has God given to you to satisfy those thirsts? From what well did you drink? To whom have you offered living water? Or who has come to drink from your well?

PRAYER: Loving God, you satisfy your people's thirst with drink from the river of grace of your Son. Grant that I may drink from the fountain of life and live with you for ever. Hear me through Jesus Christ, my Lord. Amen.

Water and Blood

Scripture: Jesus knew that he had now finished his work. And in order to make the Scriptures come true, he said, "I am thirsty!" A jar of cheap wine was there. Someone then soaked a sponge with the wine and held it up to Jesus' mouth on the stem of a hyssop plant. After Jesus drank the wine, he said, "Everything is done!" He bowed his head and died. One of the soldiers stuck his spear into Jesus' side, and blood and water came out (John 19:28–30, 34).

Reflection: Although it is common biology, most people are not aware that they carry a type of plumbing system within them called the lymph system, the Latinized form of the Greek "nymph" meaning "water goddess." Lymph is a fluid that bathes the tissues, passes into the lymphatic channels and ducts, is discharged into the blood stream, and consists of a liquid portion resembling blood plasma and contains white blood cells but normally no red ones.

Unique to John's Gospel is the story of a soldier piercing Jesus' side with a spear and water and blood flowing out. From our contemporary biological understanding, the author may have more accurately written that lymph and blood emerged. But, as is always the case in John's Gospel, there is more to be seen than just lymph and blood dripping from a wound in Jesus' side.

The astute reader will remember that in chapter two of the gospel, we read a unique Johannine story about Jesus attending a wedding in Cana and "there were six stone water jars" (2:6) that, after they were filled to the brim, became the best wine of the celebration. Six is an incomplete number. Therefore, we have been searching for that seventh jar throughout the gospel. It will complete the wedding feast.

We discover it at the cross, where it is "a jar of cheap wine" (19:29). As soon as Jesus drinks the wine, he dies. His work is completed and the wedding feast, the union of God and people, is consummated. Furthermore, like the blood of the passover lamb sprinkled on the doorposts and lintel of the Israelites' homes, and like Moses sprinkled the Israelites and the altar, representing God, with the blood of bulls in order to ratify the covenant, Jesus, a new passover lamb, has instituted a new covenant with his own blood. While it involves a sacrifice, its focus is on the wedding feast with God.

Nature Spirituality

The author of the Fourth Gospel also wants to bring together what he considers to be the two most important ways his church could celebrate the new covenant. The blood and water flowing from Jesus' side reminds us of God opening the first man's side, removing a rib, and creating a woman out of it. In a way of speaking, Adam gave birth to Eve. In John's Gospel, Jesus gives birth to the church, his bride, through water (baptism) and blood (eucharist).

Indeed, we are initiated into the new covenant through baptism, a rebirth in water and Spirit (Nicodemus), an act of opening the well and watching it overflow as living water (Samaritan woman). We renew our marriage vows to Christ before God every time we gather to eat the living bread (Christ's body) and drink the wine (Christ's blood). We feast on the food that fills us with God's life, God's presence. Being made whole, we discover that "there are three who tell about" God's deed at the cross. "They are the Spirit, the water, and the blood, and they all agree" (1 John 5:7–8). With these three—all signs of life—we are filled with eternal life.

JOURNAL: Through what experiences of your life have you discovered that you were made whole (found the seventh jar of wine)? What role did water, blood, and Spirit play in bringing you to wholeness? What other signs of God's presence were there?

PRAYER: Mighty God, you summon the earth from the rising of the sun to its setting, and you fill all your creation with life. Instill in me a spirit of thanksgiving for the water and blood of Jesus Christ, your Son, I share. May you be praised for ever and ever. Amen.

3

Earth

> Let the earth bless the Lord;
> let it sing praise to him and highly exalt him forever.
> Bless the Lord, mountains and hills;
> sing praise to him and highly exalt him forever.
> Bless the Lord, all that grows in the ground;
> sing praise to him and highly exalt him forever.
>
> —Daniel 3:74–76

Earth Created

Scripture: In the beginning God created the heavens and the earth. The earth was barren, with no form of life.... When the LORD God made the heavens and the earth, no grass or plants were growing anywhere. God had not yet sent any rain, and there was no one to work the land (Genesis 1:1–2a; 2:4b–5).

Reflection: In a fraction of a second, called "in the beginning," God created the earth—soil, dust, ground, turf. That is the one point upon which both stories of creation in the Hebrew Bible (Old Testament) Book of Genesis agree. The origin of all that exists began with God creating the earth. After that each story of creation takes its own path—one describes the rest of creation taking six days and God resting on the seventh, while the other describes the creation of man from soil and woman from man's rib in a garden.

The prophet Isaiah records God as saying: "I am the LORD God. I created the heavens like an open tent above. I made the earth and everything that grows on it. I am the source of life for all who live on this earth, so listen to what I say" (Isaiah 42:5). The prophet's words compare the earth to a tent, which, of course, is not unusual considering that ancient people lived in tents.

We often go looking for God when the earth itself is a manifestation of God's presence. Maybe because we live on the earth, we are too close to it. Or maybe we get too caught up in using the earth to pay attention to the divine present in it. With a few minutes of reflection, we begin to see that from the days of our childhood we are draw to the earth. Small children love to play in a sandbox or grab soil, toss it into the air and all over themselves, or put it into their mouths. As they grow older they may participate in making mud pies. Many adults plan their spring gardens throughout the winter months, so that as soon as the danger of frost is past they can get their hands into the soil and plant the seeds. Even replanting or transplanting a house plant puts us in contact with the earth through potting soil.

There is something about earth that draws us to itself. We relish getting that soil under our fingernails and touching that of which we are made. The Creator draws us to the dust because God has left God's presence in the earth. When we touch soil, we feel that which the Creator touched and experience the energy of the beginning all over again. In fact, the earth continues to draw us to itself, until one day we sleep for ever under a blanket of its protection.

The third planet from the sun is our home, but it is also a manifestation of the Creator. Just as the earth is barren without God's life coursing through it, so, too, are we if we do not remain in contact with source of all life.

JOURNAL: When was the last time you got your hands dirty with soil? How did you feel? In what ways was God present to you? Make a list of the ways that the earth nourishes your life. In what ways do you nourish the life of the earth?

PRAYER: Creator God, how majestic is your name in all the earth! The work of your hands I see in the sun, the moon, and the stars. Be ever mindful of me and guide me to use all you have created for your glory. Hear my prayer through Jesus Christ, the Lord. Amen.

People of Earth

SCRIPTURE: God said, "Now we will make humans, and they will be like us." So God created humans to be like himself; he made men and women. God looked at what he had done. All of it was very good!

The LORD God took a handful of soil and made a man. God breathed life into the man, and the man started breathing. The LORD God said, "It isn't good for the man to live alone. I need to make a suitable partner for him." So the LORD God made him fall into a deep sleep, and he took out one of the man's ribs. Then after closing the man's side, the LORD made a woman out of the rib (Genesis 1:26a, 27, 31a; 2:7, 18, 21–22a).

REFLECTION: Just as there are two stories of the creation of the earth in the Hebrew Bible (Old Testament) Book of Genesis, so are there two accounts of the creation of people. The first one focuses on men and women as images of God; they are like God. The second one portrays God as a potter, who first fashions a man from the soil of the earth and then, using a rib from the man, builds a woman out of it. As God sits on his throne, God builds people and things from clay, much as a potter sits at the wheel turning pots and jars.

In either account of the creation of people, the focus is on human beings as manifestations of God. We can say that we are icons, sacred images of God. Like mirrors, when we look at each other, we see God, who has signed each piece of work, each person, with divine life. To honor and to respect every human being is to recognize that he or she reflects the divine presence. That is why we strive to protect the basic human dignity of every person.

Both stories of creation also point to the equality of the sexes. In the first account, God makes men and women together and declares both of them to be very good. In the second account, even though woman is built from a rib taken from man, she is his equal. Together man and woman reflect the divine image. A painting hanging in a museum in Scotland best represents the unity of man and woman as a manifestation of God. A large person possessing both female and male characteristics sits on a bench holding a smaller person in each hand. Upon close examination, we see one individual is a man and the other is a woman. They image the equality and unity of their creator. Both are equally dust of the earth. Both are created by the God who is both male and female.

The Creator, who has left God's imprint upon us, reminds us that that which is earth is not all there is to us. There is much more. Paul once told the Corinthians: "The first man was made from the dust of the earth, but the second man came from heaven. Everyone on earth has a body like the body of the one who was made from the dust of the earth. And everyone in heaven has a body like the body of the one who came from heaven. Just as we are like the one who was made out of earth, we will be like the one who came from heaven" (1 Corinthians 15:47-49).

We retain our earthy status, while we have gained a heavenly status through the incarnation of God's own Son. Out of flesh, dust, Jesus, the one from heaven, was made. He made us realize our divine dignity by becoming one like us. God was so pleased with his work that once Jesus died, God raised him to new life. That is the same new life our dusty bodies await.

JOURNAL: What makes you realize your earthy status? What makes you realize your divine status? What people particularly manifest God to you? To whom do you think you reveal God?

PRAYER: Mighty Lord, from everlasting to everlasting you are God. At the end of my days I will return to the dust from which I came as I await your gift of new life. Teach me to count my days that I may gain a wise heart through Jesus Christ, your Son, who is Lord for ever and ever. Amen.

Tower of Earth

SCRIPTURE: At first everyone spoke the same language, but after some of them moved from the east and settled in Babylonia, they said: Let's build a city with a tower that reaches to the sky! We'll use hard bricks and tar instead of stone and mortar. We'll become famous, and we won't be scattered all over the world. But when the LORD came down to look at the city and the tower, he said: These people are working together because they all speak the same language. This is just the beginning. Soon they will be able to do anything they want. Come on! Let's go down and confuse them by making them speak different languages—then they won't be able to understand each other. So the people had to stop building the city, because the LORD confused their language and scattered them all over the earth. That's how the city of Babel got its name (Genesis 11:1–9).

REFLECTION: When an infant is first learning to speak, he or she is often said to babble, to utter meaningless or unintelligible sounds. Not being able to understand another person's language sounds like babbling to the hearer. A question mark appears on the listener's face as he or she attempts to interpret the babble, to understand what the other is saying to some degree.

The story of the building of the tower of Babel in the Hebrew Bible (Old Testament) Book of Genesis reveals that God is the origin of babble. From God come all languages. Or, in other words, every language is a manifestation of God. The various ways that people communicate on the earth reveal the myriad possibilities of communication that exist in the Creator of all languages.

That is why the tower made of hard bricks, sun-dried mud, is never finished. Those who intended to build something that would reach to the sky wanted to get in closer proximity to God, who in ancient cosmology lived above the dome of the sky, so as to communicate better with God. The story tells us that God came down to the earth. People cannot reach

God. God makes contact with people—in varied ways, such as multiple languages—to reveal that God is present on the earth.

By confusing their single language with multiple tongues God challenges people not to be single-minded in their perspectives. God does not live above the earth any more than God lives on the earth or under the earth. God speaks no single language any more than God communicates through various tongues. God is interested in building cities and living with people no more than God is concerned with a nomadic people and living in a tent, like they do.

In our world of communication overload, we can build our own earthen tower and isolate ourselves in it from everyone else. We cannot communicate because we speak but one language. We tend to believe that we have all the answers to all the questions. What we discover sooner or later is that a work-stoppage occurs on our tower and, ultimately, it collapses. God is present confusing us, making us aware of the plurality of languages that God speaks and the multiple ways that God sees. We are challenged to speak, to see, and to understand as God does. When we do, we are closer to God than we could get in any earthen tower.

Journal: What single language have you recently discovered yourself speaking (that is, of what bias have you become aware)? What tower were you building? In what ways did God confuse you? What new language did you learn to speak? In what ways was God present to you?

Prayer: Eternal God, listen to my prayer. From the end of the earth I call to you for you are my refuge, a strong tower. Let me take refuge under the shelter of your wings. I ask this in the name of Jesus Christ, the Lord. Amen.

Altar of Earth

Scripture: The LORD told Moses to say to the people of Israel: Build an altar out of earth, and offer on it your sacrifices of sheep, goats, and cattle. Wherever I choose to be worshiped, I will come down to bless you. If you ever build an altar for me out of stones, do not use any tools to chisel the stones, because that would make the altar unfit (Exodus 20:22a, 24–25).

Nature Spirituality

REFLECTION: Making an image of God is forbidden among the Israelites because their God cannot be imagined. To see God speak from heaven is to hear thunder and see lightning. No representation of God can be made; no picture can be painted; no stone or wood carved. In modern understanding, if a photograph or a video tape was made, it would turn out blank. God is invisible.

God's invisibility creates a problem for a people who want to have some assurance that their God is with them. So, God instructs the people that they can get close to God in worship by building an altar of earth. The ground is holy, as Moses had found out previously when he was told to remove his sandals, because it bears the fingerprints of the Creator. The altar of earth is not permanent and reflects the wondering stage of Israel's existence. Anywhere the people stop on their journey they can build an altar and be assured that God is present with them.

Once they cease being a nomadic people and begin to settle into cities, they built altars of stone to God. A stone altar is permanent and signifies God's permanent dwelling with people. However, the stones must be unhewn, not touched with any human instrument. They remain as they were created by God, pristine, pure, solid. As a type of earth, the stone altar is a sign of the permanence of God's presence.

While statues, icons, and pictures exist of Jesus, Christians seldom attempt to picture the invisible God. Michelangelo's painting on the ceiling of the Sistine Chapel of the old man with his finger extended to a younger man is about as close to imaging God as we have come. But we still build altars.

An altar of earth may be disguised as a garden in which the tiller plants vegetable or flower seeds, is brought closer to the God who created the ground, and recognizes the divine presence in the fruit of the soil. The altar may be a favorite camping spot along a river or in the mountains where the person recognizes holy ground and worships the God who made it. Some homes are earthen altars, especially those constructed out of adobe or some other type of mud product or stone. Those who live in them recognize the presence of God in the structure that protects them from the elements. Nomadic or permanent, our altars of earth signify God's presence with us.

JOURNAL: Where have you built altars of earth? For each identify if it was nomadic or permanent. How did each signify God's presence with you? What sacrifice did you offer on each altar? How did the sacrifice remind you of your dependence upon God?

Prayer: Invisible God, you reveal your presence through the altars your people build. Open my eyes to see you everywhere and praise you through Jesus, your Son, who lives and reigns with you and the Holy Spirit, one God for ever and ever. Amen.

Swallowed by Earth

Scripture: Moses said to the crowd, "If these men die a natural death, it means the LORD hasn't chosen me. But suppose the LORD does something that has never been done before. For example, what if a huge crack appears in the ground, and these men and their families fall into it and are buried alive, together with everything they own? Then you will know they have turned their backs on the LORD!" As soon as Moses said this, the ground under the men opened up and swallowed them alive, together with their families and everything they owned. Then the ground closed back up, and they were gone (Numbers 16: 28a, 29–33).

Reflection: We know that the more often a story is told the more it evolves because people keep changing and seeing the events narrated from a different perspective. To see how true this is all one would have to do is to record the family stories told at two successive Thanksgiving Day gatherings and compare them. The elements of similar stories would remain the same, but the interpretation would be different because the story-tellers have changed over the year.

The same is true of the account of the earthquake in the Hebrew Bible (Old Testament) Book of Numbers. Korah, Dathan, Abiram, and On decided to rebel against the leadership of Moses and the priesthood of Aaron. Moses is confident that God has chosen him to lead the people and that God has chosen Aaron as their priest. The severe earthquake which selectively swallows up the four men, their families, and all their belongings demonstrates that God is in charge and that God has chosen Moses and Aaron to lead the people.

In the ancient world, people did not have the geological understanding that we have today. They had not yet heard of tectonic plates which grate against each other and slip, causing the earth to quake or a volcano to erupt. Peoples of the past thought that the shaking of the earth was caused by God, and it indicated God's displeasure with people. The epitome of God's dissatisfaction is the earthquake, which swallows up those who have rebelled or sinned. It serves as a warning to readers that the same will happen to them if they instigate a rebellion against those whom God has chosen to lead.

There was no doubt in people's mind that God's power was manifest in the shaking of the earth. Only God could be strong enough to shake the foundations of the world.

God continues to be present in earthquakes today in our lives. Anytime we are shaken to our core we can be sure that God is present causing change in our lives, leading us where we would prefer not to go. The loss of a job causes an earthquake. The death of a child shakes us to our depths. A son or daughter decides that the church in which we raised him or her is not the best anymore. We are shaken. If we can permit the quake to widen our view, to change our perspective, we can avoid being swallowed by it. If we fail to respond to the challenge, we can be swallowed by the quake. Those who experience the earthquake and remain faithful to God throughout it do not fall into the cracked earth. They continue their journey to the promised land, like the Israelites, who continued to follow Moses and Aaron.

Journal: What recent earthquake have you experienced? What crack appeared in your life? How did you first respond to it? How did you remain faithful to God through it? In what ways was God present to you in your earthquake?

Prayer: Lord God, remember me and deliver me from all harm. Do not let the earthquakes of my life shake my faith in you, Father, Son, and Holy Spirit, one God for ever and ever. Amen.

Wagon of Earth

Scripture: [After he had been cured of his leprosy,] Naaman and his officials went back to Elisha. Naaman stood in front of him and announced: "Now I know that the God of Israel is the only God in the whole world. Sir, would you please accept a gift from me. If you won't accept a gift, then please let me take home as much soil as two mules can pull in a wagon. Sir, from now on I will offer sacrifices only to the LORD" (2 Kings 5:15, 17).

REFLECTION: Naaman, the commander of the Syrian army, had leprosy, a skin disease. After approaching Elisha and being told to dunk himself in the Jordan River seven times, Naaman at first rejected the idea. Later, after his staff suggested that he at least try it, he went to the Jordan, where he was cured. God, signified by the complete number seven, the times Naaman plunged into the water, healed him of his leprosy.

Once he was healed, Naaman returned to Elisha and professed his faith in the God of Israel. Naaman was a Syrian, a pagan, who, through his healing, is converted to worship the only God of the whole world, the one Elisha and the people of Israel adore. If that were not astounding enough, he wanted a wagon of Israel's earth to take home with him so that he could worship God on Israel's soil no matter where he might be.

Naaman believed that Israel's earth was holy ground. By hauling a wagon load back to Syria, he could remain in contact with Israel's God. The presupposition to Naaman's request is that God can only be worshiped in Israel. By taking home some of Israel's soil, Naaman takes home some of Israel and is able to worship its God where the army commander lives.

Most people do not attempt to bring home some of the holy ground where they discover God's presence, although some do carry small bottles of sand from the seashore or a small stone from a mountain peak or a riverbed. We recognize that God can be worshiped anywhere and at anytime and is not limited to Israel. However, we do maintain those holy-ground places and frequent them as often as possible because God was present to us there.

Sacred earth may be a national park or a cross-country trail. It may be a beach or a forest or a spot in your back yard. For some people a vegetable or flower garden is holy ground, while for others the cemetery where their loved ones are buried is sacred earth. Deep down in our inner selves we believe as Naaman did. There is only one God. And we want to get as close to that God as possible by worshiping God on sacred earth.

JOURNAL: What do you consider to be holy ground? Make a list of places and for each identify how you have discovered God's presence there. Also identify how you worshiped God in each place. Have you ever brought home any holy ground? If so, what did you bring home and from where?

Nature Spirituality

PRAYER: God of all the earth, you guide all people with your wisdom and make them aware of your presence. There is nothing on earth that I desire other than you. Fill me with your life through Jesus Christ, the Lord. Amen.

Promise of Earth

SCRIPTURE: . . . David instructed Asaph and his relatives for the first time to sing these praises to the LORD: We must never forget his agreement and his promises, not in thousands of years. God made an eternal promise to Abraham, Isaac, and Jacob when he said, "I'll give you the land of Canaan" (1 Chronicles 16:7, 15–18).

REFLECTION: Asaph, the leader of King David's group of musicians and singers chosen from among the Levites, learned that by singing about God's promise of land, the Israelites would not forget—and neither would God. Several times the Hebrew Bible (Old Testament) Book of Genesis records God's promise to Abraham: "The LORD said to Abram: Look around to the north, south, east, and west. I will give you and your family all the land you can see. It will be theirs forever!" (13:14–15); "The LORD said to Abram, 'I brought you here from Ur in Chaldea, and I gave you this land'" (15:7); "I will give your descendants the land..." (15:18); God said to Abram: "I will always keep the promise I have made to you and your descendants, because I am your God and their God. I will give you and them the land in which you are now a foreigner. I will give the whole land of Canaan to your family forever, and I will be their God" (17:7–8).

God's promise of land to Abraham becomes the motivation for the people to claim the land and destroy its previous inhabitants, their justification for doing so, and their hope of returning when they are exiled from it. Owning a small plot of property may be important to us, but it pales in comparison to Israel's claim, based on God's promise to Abraham, to the land of Canaan.

Because of God's promise of earth to Abraham and his descendants, three groups of people continue to fight for the land of Israel. The Jews claim it by right of the promise God made to Abraham and his descendants—particularly Isaac, Abraham's younger son, and by right of conquest through war in the twentieth century. Moslems claim the same land by right of the promise God made to Abraham and his descendants—particularly Ishmael, Abraham's elder son, and by right of conquest in the seventh century. Christians claim the land by right of the crusaders' conquest in the twelfth and following centuries. Thus, the promise of earth made to Abraham and his family forever has become the promise of war between the three groups of people who worship the same God: Jews, Christians, and Moslems.

The ownership of land, no matter how small or large the parcel may be, offers us security. In our possession we have a piece of the earth, and that enhances our economic and self-worth. The goal that most people set for themselves in our culture is to live temporarily in an apartment, and, then when they have saved enough money, to buy a home. Buying a home is synonymous with owning land. To protect our property and to mark clearly where it begins and ends, we erect barriers, usually fences, which keep us in and keep others out. When owning a plot or an acre of land is not possible, some people spiritualize the idea and say that heaven is our promised land.

Our drive to own some land can blind us to the fact that God owns the land. All earth (and planets and solar systems) belongs to God. The Israelites received their land, and under the reign of King David the borders were extended to their farthest bounds ever in their history. After being taken away to Babylonian captivity, the people returned to their land. The promise of land was extended to the Moslems, who worship the same God, through Ishmael. Then, because of their desire to have access to the places where Jesus walked and talked, Christians, who worship the same God as the Jews and Moslems, became heirs to the promise of the land.

The lesson we need to learn is that God really owns the land and leases it to people. The challenge is for people—in this case Jews, Moslems, and Christians—to live together in harmony and realize that God has fulfilled the promise of earth to people over and over again. We do not need to have a deed that gives us title to a piece of land. We have God's promise. That should unite us and be enough. When we stop focusing on the land and focus on the promise, we recognize the presence of the God who owns all of the earth.

Nature Spirituality

> **JOURNAL:** What land do you own? How is it protected? In what ways has God's promise of the earth been kept for you? How does knowing that Jews, Moslems, and Christians worship the same God help you to realize that it's God's promise that continues to be kept and not the fact of who controls the land that is important?
>
> **PRAYER:** Lord my God, I give thanks to you and call on your name. Be mindful of the covenant you made with Abraham and his descendants and grant peace to the land held sacred by Jews, Moslems, and Christians. Hear my prayer through Jesus Christ, the Lord. Amen.

Slaves of Earth

> **SCRIPTURE:** . . . A new king came to power. He did not know what Joseph had done for Egypt, and he told the Egyptians: There are too many of those Israelites in our country, and they are becoming more powerful than we are. The Egyptians put slave bosses in charge of the people of Israel and tried to wear them down with hard work. The Egyptians were cruel to the people of Israel and forced them to make bricks and to mix mortar and to work in the fields (Exodus 1:8–9, 11a, 14).
>
> **REFLECTION:** After a famine in the land of Canaan, Jacob took his eleven sons to Egypt to join his twelfth son, Joseph, who earlier was made governor there by the pharaoh, and to live off the food supplies Joseph had the foresight to store for the years of hardship. But as the Israelites continued to multiply, they became a threat to the Egyptians and were reduced to the status of slaves of the earth. By controlling the people in this manner, the Egyptians not only had free labor, but they insured themselves against any slave rebellions.

But being slaves of the earth is exactly where the Israelites got their strength, even though they did not at first recognize it. It was not strength in numbers, but it was a strength that comes from God. Their daily contact with the earth through gathering straw, making mud bricks, mixing mortar, and working in the fields connected them to the God from whom they were slipping away. Quietly, God was working through the Israelites to prepare them for the birth of Moses and his leadership which would guide them from slavery to freedom and back to the land promised to Abraham, Isaac, and Jacob.

What the Israelites learned, we, too, learn. We need time away from our homeland, our home turf, to reconnect with our God, who enables us to see our slavery and the freedom we desire. Maybe it is a drinking problem we have. We become a slave to the bottle. God sends people into our lives who guide us to a treatment center with its acres of grounds where we are set free from our slavery. We will never be cured completely, but we will always be in the process of gaining more and more freedom. Maybe we recognize that the alcoholic beverages which pushed us into treatment are made from the fruits of the earth.

People with poor health of whatever kind can become slaves to their bodies. They need a trip away from themselves to make contact with the earth. So, the therapy becomes weaving, house plants, pottery, painting, music, anything of the earth that lifts them out of their slavery. As they focus more and more on their skills, they experience healing. Maybe they recognize that their bodies are made of earth, and God was with them all along.

Egypt is less a place and more of a state of existence. When we are out of contact with God, we have moved to Egypt and become slaves of the earth. When we recognize that God is the source of our life and strength, that God owns the earth, we are sent a liberator who leads us to freedom. Then we become free men and women of the earth, recognizing that even in our brick-making and mortar-mixing that God is present with us. God works through the earth to bring us home.

JOURNAL: When have you become a slave of the earth? Who made you aware of your slavery? How were you set free? How was God at work keeping you in contact with the earth? How did God bring you home?

PRAYER: Eternal God, at a time of famine you sent your servant Joseph, sold as a slave, to nourish your people with food. Israel came to Egypt and you made him stronger than his foes. Strengthen me in my resolve to recognize your presence throughout the earth and to praise you through Jesus Christ for ever and ever. Amen.

God of Earth

SCRIPTURE: ... David sang praises to the LORD: I praise you forever, LORD! You are the God our ancestor Jacob worshiped. Your power is great, and your glory is seen everywhere in heaven and on earth. You are king of the entire world, and you rule with strength and power. We are only foreigners living here on earth for a while, just as our ancestors were. And we will soon be gone, like a shadow that suddenly disappears. Our LORD God, we have brought all these things for building a temple to honor you. They belong to you, and you gave them to us (1 Chronicles 29:10b–12a, 15–16).

REFLECTION: David, the greatest king of Israel, recognized that God was greater than he was. While we at first may not find that too earth-shattering, in a polytheistic society in which the ruler of the nation "created" or declared what gods were to be worshiped David's praise of the one God who created and owns everything is astounding. In his hymn of praise, the king focuses on two aspects of God: permanency and ownership of all things.

Unlike people, who are foreigners living on the earth for only a short time, God is permanent. The short life-span of people is contrasted to the eternity of God. We are gone, like a shadow that disappears at noonday, but God remains forever.

Unlike people, who are dependent upon God to create everything, God is independent. All things are owned by God, who gives them to us so that we can give them back to God. We may think that we own something, but whatever we have we got as a gift from God.

Both of these aspects of God contribute to the fact that David was not able to build the Jerusalem Temple, but had to leave it to his son and heir to the throne, Solomon. David's lifetime was too short, even though he reigned as king for forty years. He died before the Temple could be started, even though he had prepared for it by storing huge amounts of materials. But the materials for building a house for God were God's to begin with. A throne for God would be erected when God was ready. Why did the God who owned everything need a house built out of that which was God's anyway?

David's words of praise do well to remind us of our place in the great scheme of things. As the cliché so aptly states, we are here today and gone tomorrow. We take ourselves too seriously. We are not as important as we think we are. After eighty years, give or take some, we, the foreigners that we are, disappear. Maybe someone remembers us for a few years, but once the obituary is printed and the eulogy is delivered, that's it.

Likewise, we make too important the ownership of things. Most people collect something—dolls, plates, thimbles, stamps, coins, bank accounts. We keep building bigger homes to store the furniture we own. A three-car garage is filled with almost anything except a car in every space. Attics overflow. And what can't be kept inside the house or garage makes its way to an outdoor storage shed. What we treasure and keep will be given away or thrown away by someone else some day. Items may have our name on them, but they all belong to God. The money we saved will be spent by another.

Our God of the earth reveals God's glory everywhere in heaven and on earth, even in our transitory existence and in God's lending us the use of a few of all the things God owns. Like David, we can only praise the God of earth for being present to us through our impermanence and poverty.

JOURNAL: Do you think you live more with the presupposition of your permanence or impermanence on the earth? Explain. What are five of your prized possessions? For each identify how it was a gift from God and how God owns it. In what ways do you see God's glory, presence, in your impermanence and your poverty?

PRAYER: God of all the earth, all comes from you and all will return to you at the end of time. May I use wisely all that you have entrusted to me. Grant that I may praise you for ever in your domain, where Jesus is Lord. Amen.

Temple of Earth

SCRIPTURE: Solomon's workers began building the temple in Jerusalem on the second day of the second month, four years after Solomon had become king of Israel. Solomon had the inside walls of the temple's main room paneled first with pine and then with a layer of gold, and he had them decorated with carvings of palm trees.... He used precious stones to decorate the temple, and he used gold ... to decorate the ceiling beams, the doors, the door frames, and the walls. Solomon also had the workers carve designs of winged creatures into the walls. The most holy place . . . and its walls were covered with almost twenty-five tons of fine gold (2 Chronicles 3:1–2, 5–8).

Reflection: The Temple for which King David had collected building materials was erected by King Solomon, David's son and heir to the throne of Israel. The Temple was designed to take the place of the ancient tent of meeting under which rested the Ark of the Covenant. Just as the tent and Ark were signs of God's presence with people, so would the Temple be—only on a grander scale. Furthermore, just as God had lived in a tent when God's people were itinerant, now God would live in a permanent house since God's people had taken over and built cities.

To show the magnificence of God, Solomon used tons of gold, as well as precious stones, in the Temple, especially in the Holy of Holies, the innermost shrine housing the Ark of the Covenant. In the ancient world gold was as much a precious metal as it is today. Anything that people have little of, such as platinum, gold, or silver, is valued above that which people have much, such as copper, tin, or glass. So, Solomon finished the Temple with the most precious metal he had—gold. Only the best could be used for God's new house.

Likewise, the Temple was decorated with precious stones, which in the ancient world were as valuable as they are today because there were few of them. Gold rings are often set with a diamond, a ruby, or an emerald. The cut of the stone causes the reflected light to make it sparkle. And whatever sparkles draws us to admire its beauty and its preciousness.

However, if we stand back from gold's value and precious stones, we suddenly discover that both come from the earth. Gold does not fall out of the sky when lightning flashes, nor is there a pot of it at the end of a rainbow. Gold is mined from the earth. It is found embedded in rock with other minerals or in stream beds where it has been washed out of its source. Precious stones are rocks that are cut away from other minerals and polished. In most cases, unless they are polished, no one would recognize them as having any value. Thus, one of the most precious of metals as well as precious stones used to build the Temple are from the earth. No matter how much it shines, no matter how much they sparkle, gold and precious stones come from the earth, the primordial sign of the presence of God.

We need grand structures, like the first Temple in Jerusalem, to lift us out of our dailyness. The great Gothic cathedrals, such as those in England and France built in the twelfth and thirteenth centuries, guide us to higher things and enable us to soar upward towards God. But we also need to stay in contact with the ordinary, the earth, the source of whatever we craft into magnificence. The Temple Solomon built was a juncture of both. Grounded in the earth, it housed the presence of the Creator of all—God, who is greater than all that has ever been created or built.

JOURNAL: What is of value to you: gold, stones, etc.? Make a list and for each identify how the item both enables you to transcend yourself and keeps you in contact with the ordinary. How does each item serve as a sign of God's presence to you? Where have you discovered temples that are filled with the presence of God?

PRAYER: I give you thanks, God, with my whole heart, and I sing your praise. I give you thanks for your steadfast love and your faithfulness. Increase my strength of soul and make me aware of your presence. I ask this through Jesus Christ, the Lord. Amen.

Earth's Foundations

SCRIPTURE: From out of a storm, the LORD said to Job: Why do you talk so much when you know so little? Now get ready to face me! Can you answer the questions I ask? How did I lay the foundation for the earth? Were you there? Doubtless you know who decided its length and width. What supports the foundation? Who placed the cornerstone, while morning stars sang, and angels rejoiced? (Job 38:1–7)

REFLECTION: In ancient cosmology, the earth is thought of as a plate, flat in the middle with mountains all around, sitting on and supported by huge columns, called the pillars of the earth. In God's talk to Job, the foundation of the earth is the topic of God's questions. Until astronauts were able to travel away from earth and look back to see that it was a sphere instead of a plate, people could not get a view of the planet because they lived on it and were too close to it. At the time of the writing of the Hebrew Bible (Old Testament) Book of Job, God, the Creator, alone knew how the earth looked.

The metaphor employed for creating the earth in God's monologue is building an important public structure or a house. The first step in erecting any type of building is the foundation. The earth has to be leveled and concrete, stone, or some other solid material set in place before anything else can be built. The pouring of concrete or the laying of stone presupposes that one knows the dimensions for the structure, its length and width, so that the foundation is the right size for the building that will rest upon it.

One important element of the foundation in the ancient world was the cornerstones. The four corners of a structure are where the pressure points converge from the walls, the floors, the ceiling, and the roof. If the cornerstones are not set firmly and begin to sink, then the building will begin to split apart and fall down. God asks Job if he knows how the foundations for the earth were prepared and what supports them, who decided the earth's size, and who laid the cornerstones.

Of course Job cannot answer. It's not that Job doesn't know any cosmology. It's that Job cannot know how the earth was built because that information is reserved to God who was alone when the Holy One created the earth. By God's questions, Job is reminded that he is a creature, who has been created by God. No one can answer God's questions which deal with that which the Mighty One created before humankind.

God's questions shake Job's foundations. And that is the point of the monologue. Job, who is wise, is not as wise as God—a fact Job learns quickly. In our world of specialization, it is easy for us to think like Job. An expert is someone who knows more about engineering or electricity or biblical studies than anyone else. If no one else can answer a question, ask the expert. In the questions God presents to Job we are reminded that there is only one expert—God. The Holy One alone knows how the earth was created. Our theories—creationism, Big Bang, or whatever—are merely theories. We don't have the answers. The origin of the foundations of the earth is known to the Creator alone, but the earth manifests the Creator's presence.

> **Journal:** What is your cosmology? In other words, how do you picture the earth in your mind? Draw a picture of it on paper. In what ways do the unanswerable questions about the earth's origins reveal the presence of God to you?

Earth

Prayer: Creator God, from nothing you fashioned the earth and filled it with all good things. In the fullness of time you saved me through your Son, Jesus Christ, the stone rejected by the builders that became the chief cornerstone. All you do is marvelous in my eyes, and I praise and thank you now and for ever and ever. Amen.

Dust and Ashes

Scripture: Job said [to God]: No one can oppose you, because you have the power to do what you want. You asked why I talk so much when I know so little. I have talked about things that are far beyond my understanding. You told me to listen and answer your questions. I heard about you from others; now I have seen you with my own eyes. That's why I hate myself and sit here in dust and ashes to show my sorrow (Job 42:1–6).

Reflection: In religious circles, conversion is a buzz word, one that almost every person uses, but no one knows exactly what it means. Most people think of changing from one religious denomination to another or from one religion to another when they hear the word conversion. However, at its core, the word has more to do with the way we are in the world. Conversion describes a way of being in the world.

The Hebrew Bible (Old Testament) Book of Job closes with Job's conversion, the way God changed Job's being in the world. Of course, it involves the earth—in this case, dust and ashes. Job, who has maintained his innocence throughout the forty-two chapters of the book, recognizes that even though he is innocent of any wrong-doing, he is nothing but dust and ashes in God's sight. That is not meant to be demeaning, but it is meant to remind Job that he is the creature and God is the creator. Job sits in dust and ashes because he has been created out of dust and ashes. By getting in physical contact with dust and ashes, he also gets in contact with God.

The scene is paradoxical. When Job is most human, a creature of dust and ashes, he is also most divine, recognizing the greatness of the Creator who wills to share God's own life with people. Job's breakthrough comes when he declares that before he was converted he had heard about God from others. Now that his way of being in the world is changed, he has seen

God with his own eyes. Job, touched by dust and ashes, has been embraced by the presence of the divine.

Christians often get dust and ashes smeared on their foreheads on Ash Wednesday to herald the beginning of Lent as a season of conversion. But that is about as far as conversion goes. Job doesn't sprinkle dust and ashes on himself and then convert to a new way of life. No, he declares that God has so challenged him that his way of being in the world has already changed and, through the sign of dust and ashes, he demonstrates that he is more in contact with God than he ever was before.

Once God has touched us in some way, we desire to make contact with the earth. Some people feel driven to the shore of the ocean, the summit of a mountain, the sands of the desert. Others repot a house plant, till the garden, rake leaves, trim hedges, pick up trash along the highway, mow the yard. In whatever sign they choose, they demonstrate that they have had their way of being in the world altered. We seek out places on the earth, our form of dust and ashes, which connect us to the divine presence that confirms our conversion.

What Job learned is a message that still needs to be heard: Conversion is not a one-time event; it is an on-going process that lasts a lifetime. We are always in the process of being converted by God, of seeking out dust and ashes, of recognizing the divine presence in our lives, and of being propelled into more conversion, more dust and ashes, and more of God's own life.

Journal: What have been the major conversion experiences of your life? Make a list of them. For each identify how you signed the conversion with dust and ashes. For each identify how your way of being in the world changed. Also, for each describe how God was present to you through the dust and ashes.

Prayer: Compassionate God, you remember that I am but dust and ashes, that my days are like grass, that I flourish like a flower of the field, and then I will be gone. Teach me to do your will and to take delight in your presence. I ask this in the name of Jesus Christ, who is Lord for ever and ever. Amen.

Potter Works Earth

Scripture: A potter kneads the soft earth and laboriously molds each vessel for our service, fashioning out of the same clay both the vessels that serve clean uses and those for contrary uses, making all alike; but which shall be the use of each of them the worker in clay decides. With misspent toil, these workers form a futile god from the same clay—these mortals who were made of earth a short time before and after a little while go to the earth from which all mortals are taken, when the time comes to return the souls that were borrowed (Wisdom 15:7–8).

Reflection: If you have ever attended a craft fair, you have seen all types of pottery on display. Pottery plates, mugs, bowls, pitchers, trays, and goblets fill the booths of the fair. Some potters specialize in making particular items, in using a certain type of clay, in a unique design, or a single glaze. If we observe people near a pottery display, we notice that they just can't help but pick up the pieces. Pottery beckons us to touch it, to feel its smooth and rough places.

The potter sits at his or her wheel, beginning with a mound of clay, shaping it with his or her hands, building it into a vase or a bowl. If the shape spinning on the wheel doesn't match the image in the potter's mind, with a single movement of his or her hands the clay collapses in on itself and the potter begins again. Like one kneads a bowl of dough, the potter throws vessels on the wheel.

The potter's work in clay, mud, earth is what fascinates us and both draws us to watch the potter longer and to the artist's creation itself. If a plastic coffee mug, a glass one, and a ceramic one are set near the coffee pot, which one will most people use first? The one made out of clay, the pottery or ceramic one, beckons us to pick it up, to pour coffee in it, to caress it in our hands as the warmth from within permeates the clay and radiates toward us. As the author of the Hebrew Bible (Old Testament) Book of Wisdom states so clearly, we are drawn to the earth because we are made of it, and we will return to it some day.

The danger about which the author of Wisdom warns is that the creature, who fashions the pots, can turn the clay into an idol. In other words, the potter can create a god from the work of his or her hands. Wisdom cautions that the supreme potter is God, the creator of everything, including the clay out of which the potter creates, out of which the potter is created.

Therefore, it is foolish to worship clay idols. They are made by hands of clay which were made by God. Recognizing that God's presence emanates from the clay, the potter should not even think of creating an idol. To use the clay for such a purpose would not only be a misuse of it—making a god out of that which God created—but it would also imply that the potter, who is also a God-creation, has the ability to be a god.

We are not God, but we are like God when we create. And that is the message that the author of Wisdom is attempting to convey. The potter, like all people, is created by God in the image of God. When he or she sits at the wheel and makes pots, mugs, or trays, he or she is very much like God, creating like God creates. What he or she throws on the wheel manifests the presence of God, even as he or she is a manifestation of God. The clay is filled with the divine, just as we are filled with the divine presence. Like the pottery that draws us to itself, God draws us to God's self through the earth, through the potter working the earth into a vessel which we can use and which reminds us that we are created from the same element.

Journal: What types of pottery do you have in your home? Make a list. For each identify how you use it. How does each piece draw you toward it? How does each piece simultaneously connect you to the earth and fill you with an awareness of God's presence?

Prayer: Potter God, my refuge and strength, you are my help in trouble. I will not fear though the earth should change, though the mountains shake in the heart of the sea. When you utter your voice, the earth melts. Shape me ever more into your image with your Spirit through Jesus Christ, my Lord. Amen.

Earth Wears Out

Scripture: Look closely at the sky! Stare at the earth. The sky will vanish like smoke; the earth will wear out like clothes. Everyone on this earth will die like flies. But my victory will last; my saving power never ends. I spread out the heavens and laid foundations for the earth. But you have forgotten me, your LORD and Creator (Isaiah 51:6, 13a).

Earth

REFLECTION: We know that all things wear out. The engine in the car wears out after 100,000 miles or 250,000 miles. The body of the car begins to rust and wears out. The TV goes out after ten to fifteen years. Light bulbs burn out. The carpet wears out in the places where it is walked on the most. Dishes get small cracks and finally break.

The prophet Isaiah says that the heavens and the earth will wear out. And while that may be an on-going process, we have suddenly become aware of it in our own day and time. Who hasn't heard about the depletion of the ozone layer in the atmosphere? The harmful rays of the sun are getting through and cause more and more skin cancer. We keep pumping more and more carbon monoxide into the atmosphere so that some cities have daily doses of smog.

Natural resources are finite. Sooner or later the crude oil fields will run out. Farmers know that it is easy to wear out the soil, so they rotate crops or let the land lie fallow in order to give it a chance to replenish itself. Our sources of fresh water for drinking are more and more contaminated by what leeches into them.

Not only does the heaven and the earth wear out, but so too do people. We know that we are beginning to wear out when that slight pain in an elbow or knee persists. Livers wear out, hearts wear out, lungs wear out. Some people are fortunate to receive replacement parts or transplanted organs. But even with these, ultimately, the whole body wears out and dies.

Jesus understood the transitory quality of things. "Do you see these huge buildings?" he asked his disciples, referring to the temple and its other structures. "They will certainly be torn down! Not one stone will be left in place" (Mark 13:2; cf. Matthew 24:2, Luke 21:6). Likewise, he spoke about the wearing out of the heavens and earth: "The sky and the earth will not last forever, but my words will" (Mark 13:31; cf. Matthew 24:35, Luke 21:33).

In the midst of all things and people passing way, the prophet Isaiah reminds us that God does not wear out. God, who created the heavens and the earth and people, promises to be with people. In fact, that which wears out is a sign of God's presence. God, the creator, is greater than what God has made. And God will not let it pass into oblivion. It may be changed into a new form, but that does not mean it has disappeared.

The heavens, the earth, and every human being can serve as a reminder of God's glory and presence. Isaiah exhorts his readers not to forget God. The sky may disappear like smoke and the earth may wear out like clothes and people may die like flies, but God is eternal and shares that eternity with all that God has made.

Journal: Make a list of things that you own that have worn out recently. For each identify how it reminded you of God's presence. If someone from your family is recently deceased, how did he or she remind you of God's presence? Why do you think it is easier just to see things wearing out than it is to notice things as signs of God's presence?

Prayer: Eternal God, long ago you laid the foundation of the earth and the heavens. One day they will wear out like a garment, but you will endure. Be with me as I approach the day I will enter fully into your presence. Hear me through your Son, Jesus Christ. Amen.

New Earth

Scripture: I alone am the God who can be trusted. I am creating new heavens and a new earth; everything of the past will be forgotten. Celebrate and be glad forever! I am creating a Jerusalem full of happy people. Heaven is my throne; the earth is my footstool. I have made everything; that's how it all came to be. I, the LORD, have spoken (Isaiah 65:16f–18; 66:1ab, 2ab).

Reflection: All of us take delight in getting something new. If it is a new item of clothing, we try it on to see if or how well it fits. We stand in front of the mirror to see how we look in our new clothes. If it is a new car, we take it for a test drive, wax its exterior, and make sure that its interior is kept spotlessly clean. We show it to our neighbors and friends, inviting them to join us in our joy of owning a new car. Likewise, we want to test a new toaster or breadmaker. We will spend hours in front of the computer or television screen playing and watching. A new painting will beckon us to stop and admire it off and on for days. Anything new excites us.

God takes delight in creating a new heaven and a new earth, just like God created the old heaven and the old earth. The prophet Isaiah portrays God as forgetting the old past and looking forward to a new future for people. Since there is no time with God, as we comprehend it in a linear fashion, everything is always in the process of being created new and revealing the presence of the Creator. The invitation is to join in the party, to make it a celebration of happy people, as God renews the world.

The author of the Christian Bible (New Testament) Book of Revelation offered the same understanding to people near the end of the first century. He wrote: "I saw a new heaven and a new earth. The first heaven and the first earth had disappeared, and so had the sea. Then I saw New Jerusalem, that holy city, coming down from God in heaven" (21:1–2a). Isaiah's future newness was meant to instill in the Israelites the hope of returning to their land during their time of captivity. Revelation offers hope to the early followers of Jesus who were experiencing the trials and persecution of a hostile Roman empire. The author of Revelation makes it clear that God will provide a new heaven and a new earth, a place of peace, for those who remain faithful to the end.

What the authors of Isaiah and Revelation knew is that God is present in the very offer of hope to people. God is manifested in the ongoing process of the creation of heaven and earth. From our perspective of time, we can call it new. From God's no-time point of view, it is a process of renewal that never ends. Each morning sunrise and evening sunset marks a time of hope. Each spring renews us in hope. Each yearly rotation around the solar star instills hope. God is revealed in the sunrise and sunset, the spring, and the year. A new heaven and a new earth is nothing other than the divine flashing forth God's presence and filling us with a hope for the future.

JOURNAL: What new thing have you most recently acquired? What delight did it give to you? What hope did it instill in you? In what ways do the day, the seasons, and the year reveal God's presence to you? In what ways do they fill you with hope for more in the future?

PRAYER: Mighty God, by your word the heavens were made. At your command the earth came to be. Send your Holy Spirit to create me anew. Hear this prayer through Jesus Christ, your Son, who is Lord for ever and ever. Amen.

Jesus In the Earth

SCRIPTURE: Jesus said, ". . . The only sign you will get is the sign of the prophet Jonah. He was in the stomach of a big fish for three days and nights, just as the Son of Man will be deep in the earth for three days and nights" (Matthew 12:39b–40).

REFLECTION: Even though the above saying of Jesus most likely comes from a source biblical scholars call Q (for "Quelle," a German word meaning "source" and indicating material used by both the author of Matthew's Gospel and Luke's Gospel), the author of Matthew's Gospel has adjusted the image of Jonah being in the belly of the fish for three days to parallel Jesus being buried in the earth for three days. Originally, Jonah served as a sign of the repentance undertaken by the Ninevites after he preached to them. Likewise, those who hear Jesus preach should repent (cf. Luke 11:29–30).

The author of Matthew's Gospel returns to his image of Jesus being buried in the earth at the end of his passion story. He writes that "a rich disciple named Joseph from the town of Arimathea went and asked for Jesus' body. Pilate gave orders for it to be given to Joseph, who took the body and wrapped it in a clean linen cloth. Then Joseph put the body in his own tomb that had been cut into solid rock and had never been used. He rolled a big stone against the entrance to the tomb and went away" (27:57–60). Thus, the author of the gospel not only fulfills the prediction of the Son of Man being placed deep in the earth, he also sanctifies the earth by making it a womb for the body of Jesus.

After three days, the womb-like earth gives birth to the resurrection. After a strong earthquake, a sign of God's presence, the Lord's angel, another sign of God's presence, came down from heaven, still another sign of God's presence, and rolled away the stone, declaring that God has raised Jesus to new life. Like Jonah's life was preserved in the belly of the fish, a type of womb, and the fish set him free on the sea shore, a type of resurrection, so Jesus' life was preserved in the depths of the earth and God set him free from death on the earth, the shore of heaven, through the resurrection.

By such a feat, God turned tombs and graves and mausoleums into wombs and signs of God's presence. Where they had been signs of death, since in one of those places we lay the dead to rest, God transfigured them into signs of life. By his three days in the earth, Jesus turned dead burial places into holy, life-giving earth. By raising Jesus from the dead, God manifested the divine presence in the place where most people would not have looked—the tomb. While most believed that Jonah and Jesus were dead, God knew that they were alive, filled with divine life which flows through the belly of a fish and through the solid stone of a tomb.

We may not be conscious of it, but we believe that graves and tombs reveal the divine, life-giving presence. We bring flowers and place them on the grave or headstone. Cemeteries are often named "garden" or "lawn," places where life thrives. The womb-like tomb of earth receives the dead and flashes God's presence to those both dead and alive.

Journal: In what ways are graves, tombs, or mausoleums signs of God's presence to you? If you visit the burial sites of your relatives, what signs of life do you place there? When you have you felt like you have been swallowed by a fish or buried alive only to realize that you have emerged filled with life and more sensitive to God's presence?

Prayer: God of the living, I place all my trust in your promises. Make me more aware of your presence that surrounds me and lead me through death to eternal life through Jesus Christ, your Son, who lives and reigns with you and the Holy Spirit, one God for ever and ever. Amen.

Lifted Above Earth

Scripture: Jesus told the crowd, "If I am lifted up above the earth, I will make everyone want to come to me." Jesus was talking about the way he would be put to death. The crowd said to Jesus, "The Scriptures teach that the Messiah will live forever. How can you say that the Son of Man must be lifted up? Who is this Son of Man?" Jesus answered, "The light will be with you for only a little longer. Walk in the light while you can" (John 12:32–35ab).

Reflection: In John's Gospel, "lifted up" functions as a double entendre, an expression which bears more than one interpretation. Literally, "lifted up" refers to Jesus being nailed to the cross, which lifted him up from the earth. In Jesus' dialogue with Nicodemus earlier in the gospel, he told the teacher of Israel, ". . . The Son of Man must be lifted up, just as that metal snake was lifted up by Moses in the desert" (3:14), a reference to the story about poisonous snakes biting the Israelites and their healing as the result of looking upon a bronze snake mounted on a pole (cf. Numbers 21:4–9).

"Lifted up" also refers to Jesus' resurrection/ascension in John's Gospel. After dying on the cross, being taken down, and having his body placed in a tomb, Jesus was raised by God from the earth to eternal life. He returned to God, from whom he came as the Word made flesh. Earlier in the gospel, to his disciples the Johannine Jesus declared: "There are many rooms in my Father's house. I wouldn't tell you this, unless it was true. I am going there to prepare a place for each of you. After I have done this, I will come back and take you with me. Then we will be together" (14:2–3). Through his death and resurrection/ascension, Jesus is lifted up to God.

In Johannine theology, "lifted up" is synonymous with glorification, elevation to heavenly honor. God lifts up Jesus to a place at God's right hand through the cross and through the resurrection/ascension, all of which in Johannine theology takes place simultaneously. By being "lifted up" from the earth, Jesus makes the earth glow with the light of God.

That is the message of the incarnation, God becoming flesh, and the message of the cross, God dying on the instrument of capital punishment. God is not removed from the world, sitting upon a throne above the waters of the dome of the sky. In the person of Jesus God walks on the earth, taking earthly flesh, and dying an earthly death. His exaltation does not declare the earth to be a non-desirable place, but makes it holy, shining with the presence of the divine, filled with light.

All that is of earth is holy and radiates God's presence, the Johannine Jesus says, like the rays of the sun spread light and scatter darkness. People disclose the closeness of God. Every shrub reveals God's existence. Every tree is a sacred terebinth under which God can be found. On the top of every mountain God finds a home. On every shore of every ocean God's footprints are left in the sand. The earth is charged with the divine presence which once lifted up Jesus on the cross and then lifted him to glory. It is the same lifting up through death to new life that we await. Jesus is God's light showing us the way to the God who already lives with us. "Lifted up" is human language which cannot totally grasp the reality of God's presence permeating everything that is.

Earth

JOURNAL: In what ways have you experienced being "lifted up"? In other words, how have you experienced transcendence, being pulled and stretched into someone new? How important was the place where your experience of being lifted up occurred? Do you return there? If so, why? If not, why not? How is/was that place charged with God's presence?

PRAYER: Almighty God, you command the gates of Jerusalem to be lifted up that you, the Strong and Mighty, might enter. Lift up my heart and enter there to dwell until I am lifted up to be in your presence for ever and ever. Amen.

Earthen Jar

SCRIPTURE: The LORD said: Jeremiah, go to the pottery shop and buy a clay jar. Then take along some of the city officials and leading priests and go to Hinnom Valley, just outside Potsherd Gate. Tell the people that I have said: I am the LORD all-Powerful, the God of Israel, and you kings of Judah and you people of Jerusalem had better pay attention. I am going to bring so much trouble on this valley that everyone who hears about it will be shocked. Jeremiah, as soon as you have said this, smash the jar while the people are watching. Then tell them that I have also said: I am the LORD All-Powerful, and I warn you that I will shatter Judah and Jerusalem just like this jar that is broken beyond repair (Jeremiah 19:1–3, 10–11b).

REFLECTION: An unfired clay jar is a very fragile item. If grasped too tightly, it will return to the dust out of which it has been fashioned. If it has not properly dried, the mud will explode in the kiln. Through experience, the potter knows how careful he or she must be in removing the vessel from the wheel and giving it time to dry.

The potter creates the jar from earth, just like God created people from earth. The fragility of the jar is like the fragility of the people in two ways. First, they have a tendency to forget their origins as individual creatures and as nations from God. Second, they die, returning to the dust from which they came. By employing a clay jar, a type of visual aid, the prophet Jeremiah attempts to reconnect the people to God, to each other, and to the earth.

Nature Spirituality

At the time that Jeremiah is teaching, the Israelites have forgotten from whom they came. They have abandoned the God who led them from Egyptian slavery to the promised land and turned to the worship of Baal and other foreign gods in the Hinnom Valley where, among other things, they offered their children as burning sacrifices to those gods. So, Jeremiah takes the leaders to the place of their going astray and, breaking the clay jar, demonstrates the broken state of the covenant. Both individually and nationally the people have forgotten their origins.

The pieces of the smashed jar are used by the prophet to reconnect the people to their mortality. They are beyond repair, and they will die as Judah and Jerusalem fall to their Babylonian enemies. Like the potsherds of the jar, the Israelites will be scattered, never to become the vessel of a powerful nation they once were.

The words of the Hebrew Bible (Old Testament) Book of Jeremiah continue to echo in the valleys of our lives today. When we isolate our individual selves from others, we can easily forget our origins and the God who created us. We can lose touch with the rest of the world and ignore the needs of others. Our fragmented lives cause some people to fall apart, like a smashed clay jar.

We can also isolate ourselves as a nation. The troubles of the world are our troubles. The economic injustice in other countries is our problem, too. If basic human dignity and rights are not given to peoples of other nations, we are responsible. The jar will be broken, and we will pay the price.

We are of the earth. Like Jeremiah's clay jar, one day we will return to the dust from which we were created. Since that is the lot of every human being—meaning that no one will ever escape it—contact with the potsherds should enable us to maintain an awareness of God's desire that all people share in all things equally. Otherwise, foreign gods invade our lives and demand that we worship them. The irony, of course, is that those foreign gods all have feet of clay. There is only one all-powerful God who creates people and nations and the fragility of both.

JOURNAL: When have you recently forgotten your origins? What happened as a result? When do you think our nation has recently forgotten its origins? What happened or is happening as a result? In what ways does the image of a clay jar help you to reflect on the fragility of your life, the lives of others, and serve to keep you in contact with God through the earth?

Prayer: Lord, you took me from the womb and kept me safe on my mother's breast. Do not be far from me when trouble is near and there is no one to help me. From the dust of the earth raise me to the glory of the resurrection with your Son, Jesus Christ, who lives and reigns with you for ever and ever. Amen.

Earthen Vessel

Scripture: Our message is that Jesus Christ is Lord. He also sent us to be your servants. The Scriptures say, "God commanded light to shine in the dark." Now God is shining in our hearts to let you know that his glory is seen in Jesus Christ. We are like clay jars in which this treasure is stored. The real power comes from God and not from us. We often suffer, but we are never crushed. Even when we don't know what to do, we never give up. In times of trouble, God is with us, and when we are knocked down, we get up again. We face death every day because of Jesus (2 Corinthians 4:5b–10a).

Reflection: Like a clay jar holding water, each person is a vessel for God's glory. Into the ordinary earthen vessel that each of us is, God pours his treasured glory. We know that we are not worthy jars, because we are made from the dust of the earth, and we will return to it some day. But what is stored in us is not our doing; God fills us with eternal life, God's glory, grace.

As a clay jar, each person is a container for the divine. Every human, being a unique earthen vessel, manifests the myriad faces of God. Through the cracks in our jars, God shines out of us. Jesus was the best example of a clay jar containing God's glory. Filled with the divine glory, God did not let the smashing of his earthen vessel in death be its end. He was filled with light as he rose from the dark tomb.

As clay jars, we suffer physically. We experience diseases that attack our hearts, lungs, and livers. Cancerous tumors rob us of life. We suffer mentally, as people enter periods of depression or intense worry about something over which they have no control. No one of us is immune to spiritual suffering, as we wonder about our past and strive to keep our relationship with God in some order. However, no matter what the suffering, our clay jar cannot be crushed, because it is filled with God's glory.

In times of crisis, when we are not sure of what we ought to do, our clay jars may look like they are breaking. In a medical emergency people are forced to choose between two or more good procedures for another, and they don't know what to do. A fellow automobile driver needs help along the road, and we don't know if we should stop and help or not. When we aren't sure what we should do, we don't give up because we are filled with God's glory.

Even in the face of death, our clay jar remains solid. Death has no power over us. Death cannot get near that which is filled with the divine. Like Jesus, we face death and let it take its physical toll, because we believe that death is not the end. Our earthen vessel is transformed by God into a jar of light.

JOURNAL: What type of glory has God stored in you? In what ways have you suffered physically, mentally, or faced death? How did God's glory shine through your suffering? In what ways are you already being transformed by God into a jar leaking streams of light?

PRAYER: Mighty One, with light brighter than the sun you shine through my earthen vessel. Accept the prayer of thanksgiving I offer to you and give me your salvation. Hear me through Jesus Christ, the Lord. Amen.

Earthquake

SCRIPTURE: The Sabbath was over, and it was almost daybreak on Sunday when Mary Magdalene and the other Mary went to see the tomb. Suddenly a strong earthquake struck, and the Lord's angel came down from heaven. He rolled away the stone and sat on it. The angel looked as bright as lightning, and his clothes were white as snow. The angel said to the women, "Don't be afraid! I know you are looking for Jesus, who was nailed to a cross. He isn't here! God has raised him to life, just as Jesus said he would. Come, see the place where his body was lying" (Matthew 28:1–3, 5–6).

Earth

REFLECTION: The earthquake mentioned in the account of the proclamation of the resurrection in Matthew's Gospel is not the type of earth shaking that occurs when one tectonic plate shifts in its relationship to another one. However, the unique earthquake in Matthew's Gospel may be more earth-shaking that anything that can be measured on the Richter scale.

Not only does the earthquake announce the resurrection of Jesus at the empty tomb, but it also serves as the author's means of indicating that Jesus' death and resurrection were but human seconds in one divine minute. Immediately after Jesus dies on the cross, the author of Matthew's Gospel records: "The earth shook, and rocks split apart. Graves opened, and many of God's people were raised to life. They left their graves, and after Jesus had risen to life, they went into the holy city, where they were seen by many people" (27:51b–53). Then, to give credibility to such an earth-shattering moment, the author writes: "The officer and the soldiers guarding Jesus felt the earthquake and saw everything else that happened" (27:54a).

The earthquake following Jesus' death and the one preceding the women's discovery of his resurrection are designed to unite the two stories into a single moment of divine revelation. God is present giving people new life through the death of Jesus on the cross. Resurrection cannot be separated from death, as it immediately follows it. In Matthean theological understanding, the human moment of Jesus' death is the divine moment of God's glory raising all the dead to new life. The earthquake is a sign pointing toward the divine in whose presence the dead experience life.

The author of Matthew's Gospel extends the divine presence, which has the power to shake the dead awake, to all who have died. Don't expect to feel the earth quake or to see physical graves open and dead bodies walk away. Do expect to experience the divine causing earthquakes in your life. For example, when a child falls seriously ill and doctors are able to heal him or her, an earthquake occurred, and new life emerged. When a husband and wife can't solve their differences and seek the aid of a counselor, an earthquake occurs, and their marriage rises to new life. If you've ever been in a position of having to make a tough moral decision, you know that after weighing all the pieces, you had to die to some possibilities in order to live with the one you thought was best at the time. You felt an earthquake, which resulted in some type of new life.

Whatever the type of earthquake, it is a sign of God's presence with people. Sometimes, only after a good shaking, do we realize where God

Nature Spirituality

wants us to be and what God wants us to do. The earthquake of the divine presence in our lives is more earth-shaking than any shift of tectonic plates.

JOURNAL: Name three earthquakes that you have experienced in your life. What type of death was involved in each? What type of new life followed each? In what ways was God present in each?

PRAYER: God, you are my refuge and strength, a helper in time of need. I will not fear, though the earth should change, though the mountains shake in the heart of the sea. You are always with me leading me through death to life. All praise to you, Father, Son, and Holy Spirit, one God, for ever and ever. Amen.

 4

Fire

Jesus said,
"Whoever is near me is near the fire,
and whoever is far from me is far from the kingdom."
—The Gospel of Thomas 81:1–2

Raining Fire

SCRIPTURE: The sun was coming up as Lot reached the town of Zoar, and the LORD sent burning sulfur down like rain on Sodom and Gomorrah. He destroyed those cities and everyone who lived in them, as well as their land and the trees and grass that grew there. On the way, Lot's wife looked back and was turned into a block of salt. That same morning Abraham got up and went to the place where he had stood and spoken with the LORD. He looked down toward Sodom and Gomorrah and saw smoke rising from all over the land—it was like a flaming furnace (Genesis 19:23–28).

REFLECTION: When reading the story about the destruction of the cities of Sodom and Gomorrah, most people conclude immediately that it was because of the sexual sins of their inhabitants that the places were wiped out. After careful investigation, however, and placing the story in context, we discover that while there were some sexual aberrations going on, the destruction was due to the lack of hospitality shown to the two visitors, who were God in disguise—angels.

From a scientific perspective, the story looks very much like the one told several years ago about the volcanic eruption of Mount St. Helens. As the mountain literally blew off its top, it sent clouds of ash into the air and lava covered the land, wiping out forests and grass and wildlife. The whole mountain became a flaming furnace, and the stench of sulfur could be smelled miles away. The result was a lunar landscape of desolate destruction.

The ancient author of this story in the Hebrew Bible (Old Testament) Book of Genesis attributed fire's source to God. In the ancient world, the sun was fire, the source of life and destruction. Without the heat of the sun, nothing could grow on the earth. Yet, when the rays were too hot, everything shriveled from the heat. Physical fire, conceived of as flames stolen from the sun, was needed for light, warmth, and cooking, but when it got out of its boundaries, it destroyed homes, personal property, and lives. Such is God in the ancient mind: God both grows crops and causes them to wither. God both draws people together around the fire and scatters them away from it and with it. The fire of the sun or the fire of the community camp is attributed to God, its source and the sign of God's presence.

Fire is a worthy sign of the divine presence. It serves as a reminder to us that God is simultaneously approachable and non-approachable. Like we are drawn to a campfire outside or a fireplace inside, people are attracted to God. We want to know God. And yet, just as fire burns, when we get too close, in God's presence we recognize our unworthiness and need to be purified. We cannot grasp the divine. We dare not look directly into the flames. Otherwise, like Lot's wife, we'll become like the landscape after a volcanic eruption—a lunar tract of desolate destruction.

To live in the tension between approaching the flaming presence and staying away from it is a sign of human wisdom. To do otherwise is either to become like Lot's wife or to walk in darkness.

JOURNAL: What experiences in your life simultaneously drew you closer to God and repelled you away? In what ways was God like fire? In what ways have you gotten too close and been burned? stayed too far away and walked in darkness? How do those experiences help you know your place in God's presence?

PRAYER: God of fire, no one can look at you and live, and yet you invite all people to come into your presence. Purify my heart and mind and draw me into your divine fire where I will sing and praise you for ever and ever. Amen.

Fiery Sacrifice

SCRIPTURE: Three days later Abraham looked off in the distance and saw the place. He told his servants, "Stay here with the donkey, while my son and I go over there to worship. We will come back." Abraham put the wood on Isaac's shoulder, but he carried the hot coals and the knife. As the two of them walked along, Isaac said, "Father, we have the coals and the wood, but where is the lamb for the sacrifice?" "My son," Abraham answered, "God will provide the lamb" (Genesis 22:4–8).

REFLECTION: The coals had to be carried with Abraham and Isaac because they needed fire to offer their sacrifice to God. Since God was invisible and lived above the dome of the earth, burning the sacrifice made it invisible as its smoke soared upward to God above the heavens.

Fire

Although primitive peoples had discovered ways of getting a fire started to make the sacrifice, it was easier to keep a few coals from the previous day's or night's fire and carry them along than it was to start all over again.

Abraham had experienced God as fire before Isaac was born. ". . . The LORD told him, 'Bring me a three-year-old cow, a three-year-old female goat, a three-year-old ram, a dove, and a young pigeon.' . . . He cut the animals in half and laid the two halves of each animal opposite each other on the ground. But he did not cut the doves and pigeons in half. Sometime after sunset, when it was very dark, a smoking cooking pot and a flaming fire went between the two halves of each animal. At that time the LORD made an agreement with Abram . . ." (Genesis 15:9–10, 17–18a). In such an ancient covenant-making ceremony, God appears as fire to Abraham and, like any other man, deals with the patriarch as an equal.

It is no accident that three three-year-old animals are required for the ceremony. Likewise, it is no accident that it is on the third day after their departure from their camp that Abraham and Isaac discover the place where God desires that a sacrifice be offered. Three is a sacred number, indicating a theophany, a manifestation, a revelation of God to people. God had manifested the divine presence as fire to Abraham in the covenant-making ceremony. With Isaac, the incarnation of God's promise of many descendants for him, Abraham again experiences the revelation of God as fire.

Once the Lord's angel, another way to speak about God's presence, stops Abraham from offering Isaac as a burning sacrifice, "Abraham looked up and saw a ram caught by its horns in the bushes. So he took the ram and sacrificed it in place of his son" (Genesis 22:13). To a nomadic shepherd, like Abraham, a ram was a very valuable possession. He represented fertility and the propagation of the flock. In himself he carried the potential for countless lambs. By sacrificing the ram on the altar—another sign of God's presence, Abraham declares his total dependence upon God to make his descendants fruitful and as countless as the stars in the sky or the sands on the sea shore, even though he has but one son. By making the ram a burnt offering to God, Abraham also demonstrates his trust in God's promise.

Once Christians came to believe that Jesus was the Messiah and the Son of God, after reflecting on this story about Abraham and Isaac, it didn't take them long to conclude that he was like the ram offered by Abraham. He was sacrificed on the altar of the cross and became the source of life for all the peoples of the world. Christians also found a type of Christ in Isaac,

Nature Spirituality

who was saved from death. Once Jesus died on the cross, God raised him to new life.

Maybe what Abraham didn't realize is that God was with him constantly. The divine presence surrounded him. After all, he carried the fire, the coals, with him. The fire was God's presence to Abraham.

Journal: In what ways has God manifested his presence to you in fire? Is there any significance as to the day, time, or place of your experience of God? What was the sacrifice? What was the altar upon which you offered it? How do you recognize that God was present to you without you being aware?

Prayer: Eternal God, you no longer desire burned offerings or sacrifices, but you ask for a heart that trusts in your promises. Accept my prayer of praise and make me more aware of your eternal presence. All glory is yours now and for ever. Amen.

Burning Bush

Scripture: One day, Moses was taking care of the sheep and goats of his father-in-law Jethro, the priest of Midian, and Moses decided to lead them across the desert to Sinai, the holy mountain. There an angel of the LORD appeared to him from a burning bush. Moses saw that the bush was on fire, but it was not burning up. When the LORD saw Moses coming near the bush, he called him by name, and Moses answered, "Here I am." God replied, "Don't come any closer. Take off your sandals—the ground where you are standing is holy (Exodus 3:1–2, 4–5).

Reflection: How many times do parents shout to their children, "Get back!"? "Get back!" is shouted as a warning, such as don't get any closer to the edge of the cliff or you'll fall off, or don't get any further into the water or you'll drown. Sometimes, as in the case of God with Moses, parents shout "Get back!" to a child who is getting too near a fire in a stove, a fireplace, or furnace.

Fire

However, the difference with Moses is that it isn't the fire from which God wishes to protect Moses. It is the sacredness of the earth upon which he is standing. To show proper reverence, he must remove his sandals. Bare-footed Moses is truly in direct contact with the holy ground. The fire of the non-consumed burning bush, which begins as an angel of the Lord and ends as being God speaking, is a sign of God's presence on the mountain upon which God chose to live, Sinai. In other words, Moses is surrounded by the divine presence.

Moses is a curious shepherd. He leads his father-in-law's sheep and goats across the desert to get a better look at the mountain upon which people believe God to live. In that respect the God of Moses makes his presence known like the gods of other ancient peoples—on a mountain, on a place as high above the earth and as close to heaven as possible. Fire has the ability to draw curious people toward itself—even on a mountain top.

God calls the curious shepherd by name. God knows who Moses is even before Moses has a chance to speak. The God of Israel demonstrates his power over Moses immediately. To know someone's name in the ancient world is to be able to exercise some authority over him or her. It is similar to walking down the street and hearing your name called. You turn around to see who is calling you. The person naming you has the ability to make you stop and look.

Every bush is a burning bush. We just don't see the fire. Every bush can be a revelation of the presence of God. The bush doesn't even have to be on a mountain top. It may be growing in your front yard. If you are curious, move toward it, after having removed your shoes. You must be in direct contact with the holy ground. Then, listen carefully to hear your name called. Be sure to stay back so that you don't get burned by the presence of the divine.

JOURNAL: In the experiences of your life, which have been encounters with burning bushes? What curiosity did you have? Who called your name? Who told you, "Get back!"? In what ways did the fire draw you to itself?

PRAYER: Lord God, your voice flashes forth flames of fire and shakes the wilderness. Draw me close to you and strengthen me in your service through Jesus Christ, your Son, and the Holy Spirit. You are one God for ever and ever. Amen.

Nature Spirituality

Flaming Fire

SCRIPTURE: On the morning of the third day there was thunder and lightning. A thick cloud covered the mountain, a loud trumpet blast was heard, and everyone in camp trembled with fear. Moses led them out of the camp to meet God, and they stood at the foot of the mountain. Mount Sinai was covered with smoke because the LORD had come down in a flaming fire. Smoke poured out of the mountain just like a furnace, and the whole mountain shook. The trumpet blew louder and louder. Moses spoke, and God answered him with thunder (Exodus 19:16–19).

REFLECTION: A meteorologist reading the above passage from the Hebrew Bible (Old Testament) Book of Exodus would conclude that a ferocious thunderstorm struck Mount Sinai. Thunder claps echoed against the rock, lightning strikes set fires all over the mountain's face, and smoke, clouds, and fog encircled it. In fact, the account of the same event narrated in the Book of Deuteronomy sees the event from more of a meteorological point of view. Moses is portrayed as telling the Israelites: "Mount Sinai was surrounded by deep dark clouds, and fire went up to the sky. You came to the foot of the mountain, and the LORD spoke to you from the fire" (4:11–12a).

What the meteorologist doesn't see, the person who can read signs does see. It is on the morning of the third day, following two days of ritual purification, that fire descends upon Mount Sinai and "the LORD's glory looked like a blazing fire on top of the mountain" (Exodus 24:18). While it may have been a large thunder and lightning storm, the number three signifies a theophany; God is present in the thunderstorm and its accompanying clouds, lightning, and fire. The Israelites believed that the divine presence was with them, but God was to be feared because of the power demonstrated in the storm. God would destroy them, they thought, if they failed to keep the covenant.

The author of the Christian Bible (New Testament) Book of Hebrews, in exhorting his readers to faithfulness to Christ, writes: "You have not come to a place like Mount Zion that can be seen and touched. There is no flaming fire or dark cloud or storm or trumpet sound. The people of Israel heard a voice speak. But they begged it to stop.... The sight was so frightening that Moses said he shook with fear" (12:18–19, 21). The motive

Fire

to obey the God of Jesus is not fear, but the opportunity presented by God through Jesus to serve God and Jesus. The previous covenant was made on earth; the covenant made by Jesus is in heaven. The author of Hebrews says, "Our God is like a destructive fire!" (12:29), which means that the covenant established by Jesus presents a greater risk to those who ignore it than did the one sealed by Moses. The risk is greater because no one is pushed into it by fear.

The presence of God in fire is not intended to fill people with fear. Sometimes, such as when the prophet Elijah ran away to Mountain Sinai, God is not in the fire on the mountain. After experiencing the usual signs of God's presence—wind and earthquake—"Then there was a fire, but the LORD was not in the fire" (1 Kings 19:12). Elijah discovered God to be present in a "gentle breeze." In this case, God chose not to scare his prophet, but to appeal to his heart. Jesus appealed to hearts. Instead of fostering a fear of God in us, he preferred to set our hearts on fire with love and let that blaze spread over all the earth.

JOURNAL: Make a list of the properties of fire which cause you to fear it. In what experiences of your life has God been present to you as fire, such as at a campfire, a fire place, etc.? In what ways has Jesus set your heart on fire with God's presence?

PRAYER: Almighty God, I remember your wonders of old, all your work, and your mighty deeds. Thunder rolled through the skies; lightning flashed on every side; the earth trembled and shook. May every thunderstorm and fire remind me of your presence for ever and ever. Amen.

Pillar of Fire

SCRIPTURE: During the day the LORD went ahead of his people in a thick cloud, and during the night he went ahead of them in a flaming fire. That way the LORD could lead them at all times, whether day or night (Exodus 13:21–22).

REFLECTION: Because the stories contained in the Hebrew Bible (Old Testament) Book of Exodus are the product of oral tradition which involved a retelling and reshaping by successive generations in various places, not only did duplicates of stories arise and become recorded, but no two stories always agree on the details. What remains constant through the stories about the pillar of fire is that it represents God's presence with people.

First, God leads people with a cloud during the day and a fire at night. Because clouds are beyond reach, in ancient cosmology they are close to the seat of the divinity. Likewise, the fire in the sky, lightning, comes from that place above the firmament where God lives. Thus, in the minds of ancient people, the cloud and the fire come from God and represent God. Through them, God leads the Israelites where God wants them to be.

Second, God protects the people with the cloud and the fire. After arriving at the Sea of Reeds, another story-teller says, "A large cloud had . . . gone ahead of [Israel's army], but now it moved between the Egyptians and the Israelites" (Exodus 14:19b–20a). After God parted the sea, "but before daylight," God also "looked down at the Egyptian army from the fiery cloud and made them panic" (Exodus 14:24). God protects the Israelites, as they make their escape, and confounds their enemies.

Third, the cloud and fire are signs of God's presence with the people. The author of the Book of Numbers states: "As soon as the sacred tent was set up, a thick cloud appeared and covered it. The cloud was there each day, and during the night, a fire could be seen in it" (9:15–16). Then, the author explains why the cloud and fire surrounded the tent in which God chose to live with people: "The LORD used this cloud to tell the Israelites when to move their camp and where to set it up again. As long as the cloud covered the tent, the Israelites did not break camp. But when the cloud moved, they followed it, and wherever it stopped, they camped and stayed there, whether it was only one night, a few days, a month, or even a year" (Numbers 9:17–20).

The prophet Isaiah used the cloud and the fire as signs of God's presence in the Temple in Jerusalem. The Temple, the descendent of the sacred tent, became God's dwelling place with people. Isaiah said, ". . . The LORD will cover the whole city and its meeting places with a thick cloud each day and with a flaming fire each night" (4:5). The cloud and fire not only will be signs of God's presence, but they will also protect the people from their enemies, who were getting ready to storm Jerusalem as Isaiah was prophesying.

Fire

The cloud and fire of the divine presence continue to lead and to protect people today. God works through people, who lead us to new ideas, new inventions, new ways of doing old things. We are protected by seat belts, air bags, and preventive medicine—all of which comes through people. We don't have to see a physical cloud or watch physical fire fall from the sky to experience the God who is like a pillar of cloud by day and a pillar of fire by night leading us toward the divine presence, protecting us with it, and being the very one we seek.

JOURNAL: In what ways has God led you? In what ways has God protected you? What signs of the divine presence have you seen? During the Easter Vigil, the Easter candle, a sign of the risen Christ, is called a "pillar of fire." Based on the reflection above, why do you think the church calls the candle a "pillar of fire."

PRAYER: God of fire, once you protected your people Israel by spreading a cloud of light for covering during the day and fire to give light by night. Protect me with your grace that I may complete my journey, to you who live with your Son, Jesus Christ, in the unity of the Holy Spirit, for ever and ever. Amen.

Burned Offering

SCRIPTURE: The LORD spoke to Moses from the sacred tent and gave him instructions for the community of Israel to follow when they offered sacrifices. The LORD said: Sacrifices to please me must be completely burned on the bronze altar. After the bull is killed in my presence, some priests from Aaron's family will offer its blood to me by splattering it against the four sides of the altar. Skin the bull and cut it up, while the priests pile wood on the altar fire to make it start blazing. A priest will then send all of it up in smoke with a smell that pleases me (Leviticus 1:1–2, 5–7, 9).

REFLECTION: A sacrifice is something that is given away with nothing received in return. Authentic love between two people is sacrificial; each gives freely and unconditionally to the other. The love that parents have for their children is sacrificial. Parents give countless hours, money, and other resources to nurture their offspring and assist them in becoming wholesome adults. Teachers who do extra work with students, volunteers who supervise youths in after-school programs, and the others who staff service agencies sacrifice their time. They expect to receive nothing in return.

The God portrayed in the Hebrew Bible (Old Testament) Book of Leviticus requires burned offerings or sacrifices of animals. A bull, for example, a sign of strength and fertility, is to be killed in God's presence. Its blood, a sign of life, is splashed on the four sides of the altar, representing God, the source of all life. Then, the meat is cut up and burned. The smoke, because it rises up to heaven, where God was believed to sit on the Holy One's throne, carries the offering to the seat of the divinity who is pleased with its smell.

While such an animal sacrifice is repulsive to us today, in the ancient world it spoke tomes about dependency upon God for everything. God was the source of all life. That is why the life of the animal is sacred and can be taken only in God's presence. That is why the animal's blood must be given back to God by pouring it on the altar. The offering is made not to appease an angry God, but to acknowledge that all strength and fertility come from God. The animal is burned because one of God's signs is fire. The medium for making contact with the invisible God is fire, which will make the offering invisible smoke. People are as dependent upon God for everything as was the animal, and they are as connected to God, the source of all life, as was the animal.

The animal must have no flaws. The burned offering must be as perfect as humanly possible. Since God is perfect, the sacrifice must be the best that people can offer and not what is of any use to them. By requiring that they offer their best bull to God, God desires that people will be moved to offer freely the best of their lives in authentic sacrifice.

JOURNAL: What is your definition of sacrifice? What have you sacrificed recently with a hope of getting something in return? What have you sacrificed recently with no hope of getting anything in return? In what ways does a sacrifice get you more in contact with God and with other people? When you have made a sacrifice, what type of fire was present?

PRAYER: God of life, you no longer desire the burned offerings of animals, but you call me to have a sacrificial heart. Enable me to hear your call, to delight in doing your will, and to serve you all my days. Hear this prayer through Jesus Christ, the Lord. Amen.

Consumed by Fire

SCRIPTURE: Gideon went home and killed a young goat, then started boiling the meat. Next, he opened a big sack of flour and made it into thin bread. He took the meat, the broth, and the bread and placed them under the big tree. God's angel said, "Gideon, put the meat and the bread on this rock, and pour the broth over them." Gideon did as he was told. The angel was holding a walking stick, and he touched the meat and the bread with the end of the stick. Flames jumped from the rock and burned up the meat and the bread (Judges 6:19abd, 20–21ab).

REFLECTION: Once God calls Gideon to be a leader of the Israelites, God also demonstrates the reliability of the call. Gideon wants proof that it is God who is summoning him to remove all signs of the pagan gods who have invaded the land and to lead the Israelite army against its enemies. Knowing how important a sign is to Gideon, God gives him fire. Once the judge prepares his offering of meat, broth, and bread—the staples of life, at the command of God's angel, a sign of the divine presence, God's fire consumes the gifts. Just as God has "eaten" the offering with flames, so Gideon has "eaten the call" and is on fire with God's purpose.

Later in the Hebrew Bible (Old Testament) Book of Judges, a married couple experiences the all-consuming presence of God. Manoah and his wife, Hannah, have no children because she "was not able to have children" (Judges 13:2). Hannah experiences God, whom she describes to Manoah, saying, "A prophet who looked like an angel of God came and talked to me" (13:6). God tells her that she will have a son who will free the Israelites from Philistine attacks. Later, Manoah experiences God. "Please, Manoah said, 'stay here with us for just a little while, and we'll fix a young goat for you to eat.' Manoah didn't realize that he was really talking to one of the LORD's angels" (13:15–16).

The narrator of the story continues: "So Manoah took a young goat over to a large rock he had chosen for an altar, and he built a fire on the rock. Then he killed the goat, and offered it with some grain as a sacrifice to the LORD. But then an amazing thing happened. The fire blazed up toward the sky, and the LORD's angel went up toward heaven in the fire" (Judges 13:19–20a). In other words, not only is the couple given a sign of God's presence, but Manoah and Hannah are consumed by God's fire and conceive a fire-child.

The child to whom Hannah gives birth is named Samson. He, like his parents, is consumed by God's fire and, until he is captured by his enemies, frees the land of Israel from the controlling power of the Philistines "for twenty years" (Judges 16:31). Ultimately, Samson becomes a living sacrifice offered to God as he pulls down the columns of the temple of the Philistine's god during a celebration and defeats his enemies even as he is their captive. Samson's death, like the goat offered by his parents, is an offering pleasing to God.

Even the Lukan Jesus is consumed by the divine mission which has been entrusted to him. "I came to set fire to the earth, and I wish it were already on fire!" he says (Luke 12:49). In this regard he is like the one who prepared his way—John the Baptist—and who said, "He will baptize you with the Holy Spirit and with fire" (Luke 3:16c). Indeed, we have been set on fire by the message and ministry of Jesus of Nazareth, who offered himself as a sacrifice to God.

Journal: What sign of fire have you seen as a proof of your call from God? How have you been on fire with the divine presence? In what ways have you been consumed by God's fire? To what fire have you given birth, or under whom have you lit a fire? What was the sacrifice God accepted?

Prayer: God of fire, you are like a devouring flame that consumes me. Accept the offering of my life in service to you and your reign, where Jesus is Lord for ever and ever. Amen.

Fire from God

Scripture: [Elijah] used twelve stones to build an altar in honor of the LORD. Each stone stood for one of the tribes of Israel. . . . Elijah dug a ditch around the altar. . . . He placed the wood on the altar, then . . . cut up the bull into pieces and laid the meat on the wood. He told the people, "Fill four large jars with water and pour it over the meat

Fire

and the wood." After they did this, he told them to do it two more times. When it was time for the evening sacrifice, Elijah prayed.... The LORD immediately sent fire, and it burned up the sacrifice, the wood, and the stones. It scorched the ground everywhere around the altar and dried up every drop of water in the ditch (1 Kings 19:31–36a, 38).

REFLECTION: The four-hundred fifty prophets of the pagan god, Baal, and the four-hundred prophets of the pagan goddess, Asherah, didn't have a chance when they were confronted by the prophet of the God of Israel—Elijah. As the Hebrew Bible (Old Testament) First Book of Kings narrates the story, the eight-hundred fifty prophets could not get their god to accept their sacrifice. With a flair for the dramatic, Elijah instructed that his offering be doused in water and that the ditch surrounding the altar be filled with water. Thus, the fire that consumes the altar, the wood, the sacrifice, and the water is made more dramatic by the fact that everything is soaking wet.

The pagan god and goddess are not present, like the God of Israel is. Elijah taunts their prophets, saying: "Maybe [Baal's] day-dreaming or using the toilet or traveling somewhere. Or maybe he's asleep, and you have to wake him up" (1 Kings 18:27). Israel's God doesn't need to be summoned by prayer or awakened from sleep. The signs of God's presence were present even as Elijah prepared the sacrifice.

First, the meeting of the eight-hundred fifty prophets of Baal and Asherah with Elijah takes place on Mount Carmel. While it's not Mount Sinai, nevertheless it serves as a sign of God's presence.

Second, Elijah uses twelve stones to build the altar upon which to place the sacrifice. Each stone represents one of the twelve tribes of Israel, Jacob's twelve sons, God's chosen people. The twelve tribes are the incarnation of God's promise to Abraham and his son, Isaac, Jacob's father, that their descendants would be countless. The twelve stones connect the Israelites and the land to their ancestors and to the God who gave them life, freedom, land.

Third, it is a bull that is killed, cut up, and placed on the altar. A bull's blood was used by Moses to ratify the covenant between God and the people at the foot of Mount Sinai. Some of the blood was splashed on the altar and some was sprinkled on the people. Thus, God and people became related by blood. The Holy One's promise was that the Lord would be Israel's God and the people would be the Mighty One's people. The blood of the sacrificed bull on Elijah's altar reconnects the people to their God.

Nature Spirituality

Fourth, God's single prophet Elijah orders four jars of water to be filled and poured over the cut-up bull and wood and altar three times. The number three indicates a theophany, the presence of God. And not only is God present as the all-consuming fire, but the three-times filling of four jars of water equals twelve, the number of Israel's tribes. Once again, the sign is clear: God is present.

Finally, it is no accident that it is the time of the evening sacrifice that God accepts Elijah's offering through fire. The burned-up sacrifice of bull, wood, stones, and water represent the all-encompassing presence of God, who is nearer to the people than they at first could have imagined. They acknowledge God's presence by shouting: "The LORD is God! The LORD is God!" (1 Kings 18:39), and they bow down and worship their God in whose presence no other god's prophets have a chance.

JOURNAL: Recall an experience you have had of God's presence. What type of mountain were you on? What type of altar did you build? What was the sacrifice you prepared? What was the water that made the sacrifice more difficult to offer? What time of the day was it? What fire did you experience?

PRAYER: Eternal God, often in distress I have called upon you and cried to you for help. Every time you came to my aid and restored the darkness with your light. Accept the offering of my life this day through your Son, Jesus Christ, who is Lord for ever and ever. Amen.

Fiery Chariot and Horses

SCRIPTURE: Elijah and Elisha were walking along and talking, when suddenly there appeared between them a flaming chariot pulled by fiery horses. Right away, a strong wind took Elijah up into heaven. Elisha saw this and shouted, "Israel's cavalry and chariots have taken my master away!" After Elijah had gone, Elisha tore his clothes in sorrow. Elijah's coat had fallen off, so Elisha picked it up and walked back to the Jordan River. He struck the water with the coat and wondered, "Will the LORD perform miracles for me as he did for Elijah?" As soon as Elisha did this, a dry path opened up through the water, and he walked across (2 Kings 2:11–14).

Fire

REFLECTION: The Hebrew Bible (Old Testament) Second Book of Kings' story of Elijah skipping death and going straight to heaven can be called the Ascension of Elijah. The place of Elijah's ascension is important. He and Elisha cross the Jordan River to a location where the Israelites camped before they entered the promised land. The river is a boundary, separating the sacred from the secular. From the east side of the Jordan River, the secular location, the great prophet breaks the boundary separating earth and heaven and rises to the realm of the divine. Once the ascension is complete, Elisha, wielding the mantle of his protégée, re-crosses the Jordan River, re-enters the sacred, promised land, to continue the ministry of Elijah. In other words, he reseals the boundaries.

An ascension is a breaking of the boundary between earth and heaven, between people and God. An ascension serves momentarily to unite the two. To ascend is to rise, to be transformed or transfigured, to be, as it were, pulled outside of one's self, to be turned inside out, to be divinized by God. Most religions have some type of ascension story as part of the legend of one of its heroes.

Islam has its account of the ascension of the prophet Mohammed, who ascended to heaven on a horse. The Dome of the Rock shrine in Jerusalem, built in the seventh century, marks the spot where this supposedly occurred. Mohammed blurred the boundaries between earth and heaven, between people and Allah (God), and that place became sacred, a shrine, a spot of pilgrimage for Muslims.

Christianity has its ascension story. Jesus' ascension is told twice by Luke, the author of the Gospel according to Luke and the Acts of the Apostles (cf. Luke 24:50–52; Acts 1:9–10). Both accounts not only blur the boundaries between earth and heaven, but they also occur on sacred ground. In Luke's Gospel, Jesus ascends to heaven in Bethany, a village near Jerusalem and a significant location for Jesus' activity in all four canonical gospels. In the Acts of the Apostles, the ascension takes place on the Mount of Olives near Jerusalem, another significant location for Jesus' ministry in the synoptic gospels (Mark, Matthew, Luke). It is the place from which Jesus' triumphal entry into Jerusalem begins. Therefore, it is fitting for his triumphal entry into heaven. Luke prefers to keep the fire for his account of Pentecost in the Acts of the Apostles.

While there is a horse in both Elijah's ascension and in Mohammed's, that sign of power is not found in the Christian account. In fact, the prophet

Nature Spirituality

Elisha misinterprets the sign of the flaming chariot, fiery horses, and strong wind to be Israel's cavalry or part of the army when they are signs of God's presence. God descends in the sign of fire—using the common mode of transportation, a chariot pulled by horses—and unites heaven to earth in order to divinize Elijah. That's also the point of Mohammed's ascension: Allah descends to receive the prophet as he rides his horse into God's presence. The Lukan Jesus returns to the God of heaven and earth. When God breaks boundaries, heaven and earth are united and people discover themselves in God's presence.

Journal: What type of ascensions have you experienced? What was the means of transportation between earth and heaven? What were the signs of God's presence? In what ways were you changed, transformed, or turned inside out? What fire was involved?

Prayer: God of Elijah, with a flaming chariot you carried your prophet beyond the boundaries of this world. Give to me the fire of your Holy Spirit that I may always walk in your presence and one day ascend to your domain, where Jesus is Lord for ever and ever. Amen.

Purifying Fire

Scripture: . . . I [, Isaiah,] had a vision of the LORD. He was on his throne high above, and his robe filled the temple. Flaming creatures with six wings each were flying over him. As they shouted, the doorposts of the temple shook, and the temple was filled with smoke. One of the flaming creatures flew over to me with a burning coal that it had taken from the altar with a pair of metal tongs. It touched my lips with the hot coal and said, "This has touched your lips. Your sins are forgiven, and you are no longer guilty." After this, I heard the LORD ask, "Is there anyone I can send? Will someone go for us?" "I'll go," I answered. "Send me!" (Isaiah 6:1–2a, 4, 6–8).

Reflection: To purify something means to make it clean. After it is taken from a well or a river, water is purified by city waterworks, which filters sediment and micro-organisms out of the liquid and adds chlorine and/or fluoride to further guarantee that it is fit for human consumption.

Some food is purified through cooking, which takes place in or on some type of fire, such as an oven, a burner, a barbecue, a grill, or a flame from wood or gas. The process of purification provides water and food which will not cause disease or illness in those who drink and eat.

The Hebrew Bible (Old Testament) Book of Isaiah records a story about how the human prophet experienced the purifying fire of God. Isaiah's vision is an experience of God's presence. He sees flaming creatures, signs or emanations of God, each with six wings or two sets of the theophanic number three. The smoke filling the temple and the shaking of the temple are more signs of the divine presence. But these are not enough to convince the prophet that he has a mission to embrace. Because of his humanity, he is unworthy to accept the role marked out for him by God.

Isaiah needs to be purified. God obliges with purifying fire. Since it is Isaiah's voice that God wants to send to the Israelites to deliver God's word to them, one of the flaming creatures takes a burning coal and touches it to the prophet's lips. In other words, Isaiah has his mouth washed out with fire. The Holy One cleanses Isaiah with God's self, the divine presence. Then, once he is cleansed of his human limitations, the prophet readily answers the call to go to the people and speak God's word to them.

Today, God continues to purify people with fire. Sometimes lips receive the burning coal, and people are sent forth to preach about injustice caused by racism, sexism, and other societal injustices. At other times, human hearts are set on fire with compassion, and people are moved to serve others through soup kitchens, food pantries, and other types of volunteer efforts. Those people we claim as intellectual giants have most likely had their minds purified with fire. Their ideas for a better way of life for all are inspired by God.

When the divine presence purifies each of us, we, like Isaiah, have to say, "I'll go. Send me!" We are entrusted with the Mighty One's fiery words which bring purification to more of God's people.

JOURNAL: In what ways have your lips been purified by God's fire? In what ways has your heart been set on fire with compassion? In what ways has your mind been inspired by God's fire? Where or to whom did God send you? In what ways did you help others to be touched by the divine fire?

Nature Spirituality

PRAYER: Purifying God, in every age you call men and women to be on fire with your word. Cleanse my heart and mind that my lips may proclaim your mercy and justice and that my life may demonstrate your steadfast love. I ask this through Jesus Christ, the Lord. Amen.

Walk through Fire

SCRIPTURE: Descendants of Jacob, I, the LORD, created you and formed your nation. Israel, don't be afraid. I have rescued you. I have called you by name; now you belong to me. When you cross deep rivers, I will be with you, and you won't drown. When you walk through fire, you won't be burned or scorched by the flames. I am the LORD, your God, the Holy One of Israel, the God who saves you (Isaiah 43:1–3a).

REFLECTION: The only person who walks through fire known by most of us is a fire fighter. These men and women don protective clothing and oxygen equipment and walk into burning buildings to save people and pets. Some of them jump from airplanes into burning forests to put out the flames. Others walk straight into the path of a fire in order to create a break which it cannot cross. Fire fighters save and protect people from all types of fires.

In the Hebrew Bible (Old Testament) Book of Isaiah, God is portrayed as Israel's protector. Speaking for God, the prophet first reminds the reader that God is the creator both of each individual and of the nation of Israel. The very existence of each person and the community as a whole is a sign of God's enduring presence with people.

Next, the prophet exhorts the people to have no fear. The God who is present as creator is also the God who rescues and saves, the fire-fighter God. In a manner of speaking, God spreads the invisible covering of God's presence around people. If they cross rivers, they won't drown. If they walk through fire, they won't be burned or scorched. God protects what God has created. Therefore, there is no reason to fear.

Finally, the prophet reminds the people that God is not impersonal, but personal. God calls every person by name. After all, the Holy One created everyone and named him or her as belonging to God. Having a name

Fire

is but another sign of the all-encompassing presence of God. Having a name is having a personal relationship with the divine.

Isaiah attempts to make his readers aware of how surrounded they are by the divine presence as manifested in their existence, in their lack of fear, in their experiences of being rescued from water and fire, and by being named by God. God is with them, the prophet declares. God is as close to them as they are to themselves.

JOURNAL: In what ways has God protected or rescued or saved you? Through what river did God lead you? Through what fire did you walk? With what name did God call you? In what ways do you experience the divine presence surrounding you?

PRAYER: I sing to you, God. I sing praises to your name. Your protect orphans, widows and widowers, the homeless, and prisoners. Wrap me in the mantle of your grace and bring me to the fire of your presence. Hear me in the name of Jesus Christ, your Son, who lives with you and the Holy Spirit, for ever and ever. Amen.

King of Fire

SCRIPTURE: I [, Ezekiel,] saw a windstorm blowing in from the north. Lightning flashed from a huge cloud and lit up the whole sky with a dazzling brightness. The fiery center of the cloud was as shiny as polished metal, and in that center I saw what looked like four living creatures. The creatures were glowing like hot coals, and I saw something like a flaming torch moving back and forth among them. Lightning flashed from the torch every time its flame blazed up. The creatures themselves moved as quickly as sparks jumping from a fire. I then saw what looked like a throne made of sapphire, and sitting on the throne was a figure in the shape of a human. From the waist up, it was glowing like metal in a hot furnace, and from the waist down it looked like the flames of a fire. I realized I was seeing the brightness of the LORD's glory! (Ezekiel 1:4-5a, 13-14, 26-27a, 28b)

REFLECTION: When the prophet Ezekiel experiences a vision of fire, he knows that he is in the presence of the divine. The Hebrew Bible (Old Testament) Book of Ezekiel pictures God as a warrior-king, sitting

Nature Spirituality

upon a throne of sapphire, a blue translucent stone, the color of war. Omitted from the passage above is the description of the wheels beside the four living creatures, indicating that God is also imaged as standing in a war chariot.

The image of God as a warrior is not as appealing to us today as it was to Ezekiel's contemporaries, who needed a warrior God to rescue them from their enemies. But the other signs in the prophet's vision scream of God's presence with the Israelites. Here it is important to note that the signs are of nature, but cumulatively they reveal a world charged with the divine presence which arrives in a windstorm, one of nature's most powerful forces.

The bright cloud of the storm reminds us of the pillar of cloud both leading and protecting the Israelites during and after their escape from Egyptian slavery. The fiery center of the cloud with its lightning flashes and the flaming torch with its sparks echo Moses' experience of the burning bush and his call to lead his people out of Egypt to the promised land, as well as Abraham's experience of God in making the covenant.

The four living creatures are not intended to fuel the imagination to draw pictures of strange beasts, but to indicate the four cardinal points of the earth: north, south, east, and west. God's presence encompasses the whole world in all directions. The divine presence might approach from the north, but from God's point of view, humanly speaking of course, there are no directions. The divinity is all-in-all and over all.

The divine majesty can be conceived only in human form, surrounded by bright light and totally on fire. The presence of the divine is both comprehensible and incomprehensible. We need an image to which we can cling, but the very icon must be transparent. Otherwise, we risk turning the invisible God into an idol. Caught in the middle, the prophet Ezekiel chooses fire to describe the divine presence. It both draws people toward it and repels them.

While we may not have such fiery visions of God's presence as Ezekiel, nevertheless, we can experience the divine majesty in the power of a hurricane, tornado, or water spout. We are drawn into the windstorm and cautioned about getting too close. We can experience God as a flaming torch or raging fire. We are drawn toward the light and warned not to get burned.

Fire

JOURNAL: In what ways have you experienced God in a windstorm or in fire? What human metaphor or image did you use to describe your experience of the divine presence? In what ways did you experience yourself surrounded by God's presence? What both drew you toward the force and repelled you from it?

PRAYER: I shout to you, God, with loud songs of joy. You are the great king of all the earth. Accept my praises and draw me ever closer to you through the Holy Spirit who reigns with you and your Son, Jesus Christ, for ever and ever. Amen.

Fiery Human

SCRIPTURE: . . . The LORD God suddenly took control of me [, Ezekiel], and I saw something in the shape of a human. This figure was like fire from the waist down, and it was bright as polished metal from the waist up. It reached out what seemed to be a hand and grabbed my hair. Then in my vision the LORD's Spirit lifted me into the sky and carried me to Jerusalem (Ezekiel 8:1b–3b).

REFLECTION: The prophet Ezekiel is not the only Hebrew Bible (Old Testament) prophet to describe his experience of God as a fiery human or as a human being engulfed in fire. The prophet Daniel had a vision which he described as watching the eternal God take his place upon a throne. "His clothing and his hair were white as snow. His throne was a blazing fire with fiery wheels, and flames were dashing out from all around him" (Daniel 7:9–10a).

In another vision, Daniel wrote: "I saw what looked like a son of man coming with the clouds of heaven, and he was presented to the Eternal God. He was crowned king and given power and glory, so that all people of every nation and race would serve him. He will rule forever, and his kingdom is eternal, never to be destroyed" (Daniel 7:13b–14). What was for Daniel a vision of a deliverer of the Jews from Babylonian captivity, became for Christians a description of Jesus, the king who saved people from their sins and who would return seated on a throne in the clouds.

Nature Spirituality

In the Book of Daniel the author of the Book of Revelation found a good description of what he thought Jesus would look like when he returned. Daniel had written: ". . . I looked up and saw someone dressed in linen and wearing a solid gold belt. His body was like a precious stone, his face like lightning, his eyes like flaming fires, his arms and legs like polished bronze, and his voice like the roar of a crowd" (Daniel 10:5–6).

The author of the Christian Bible (New Testament) Book of Revelation combined Ezekiel's visions and Daniel's visions into one. The result was a vision of the risen Christ: "There . . . was someone who seemed to be the Son of Man. He was wearing a robe that reached down to his feet, and a gold cloth was wrapped around his chest. His head and his hair were white as wool or snow, and his eyes looked like flames of fire. His feet were glowing like bronze being heated in a furnace, and his voice sounded like the roar of a waterfall" (Revelation 1:13–15).

The fiery-human image of God in the Hebrew Bible (Old Testament) inspires the fiery-human image of the divinized Jesus or the risen Christ in the Christian Bible (New Testament). Jesus is God, the anonymous author of Revelation is making clear. Jesus is God in fiery-human form. In a manner of speaking, he was ablaze with the presence of God.

Being created in God's image and likeness, every human being glows with God's presence. Although we do not share it in the same degree as Jesus, God's Son, God has promised that the fullness of our image will be realized on the other side of death. There we will become fiery humans, totally engulfed by the divine flames of the presence of God. We will be lifted up in our spirit-state of existence and carried to the very source of all fire: God.

Journal: Besides the fiery-human metaphor for God and Jesus, what other images can you use to describe the presence of God? In what ways have you already experienced the transforming flames of God's presence? How do these experiences give you hope for risen life on the other side of the grave?

Prayer: Eternal God, how majestic is your name in all the earth! You have made me in your likeness and given to me a share of your glory. Make me a good steward of your gifts. Hear my prayer through Jesus Christ, the Lord. Amen.

Saved in Fire

SCRIPTURE: [Nebuchadnezzar] . . . ordered the furnace to be heated seven times hotter than usual. Next, he commanded some of his strongest soldiers to tie up the men and throw them into the flaming furnace. So the soldiers tied up Shadrach, Meshach, and Abednego and threw them into the flaming furnace. . . . Suddenly the king jumped up and shouted, "Weren't only three men tied up and thrown into the fire?" "Yes, Your Majesty," the people answered. "But I see four men walking around in the fire," the king replied. "None of them is tied up or harmed, and the fourth one looks like a god." Nebuchadnezzar went closer to the flaming furnace and said to the three young men, "You servants of the Most High God, come out at once!" The men were not burned, their hair wasn't scorched, and their clothes didn't even smell like smoke (Daniel 3:19–27).

REFLECTION: Most of the time we think of fire primarily in terms of its ability to consume. The flames in the fireplace make the wooden logs disappear. The sight of a fire truck parked outside of a home and smoke pouring out of the house indicates that fire has caused damage inside. After placing a body in a crematorium, fire reduces a few hundred pounds of flesh to a few pounds of calcium, which is usually referred to as "ashes."

The furnace into which Nebuchadnezzar, king of Babylon, orders the three men thrown is heated seven times hotter than usual. The number seven indicates that it is perfectly hot and also that God is present in the flames. The soldiers who toss the three men, who themselves are a theophany, a manifestation of God, are consumed by the fire. Their lives are licked away by the flames leaping out of the furnace while the lives of the three men are protectively wrapped in the flames by God, who is pictured as a fourth person, looking like a god, walking around in the furnace, much as God walked in the garden of Eden in the cool of the day, with the three men.

Nebuchadnezzar believes that he is in charge of the world. After all, he had conquered much of the known world in the fifth century BCE. He had every right to believe that he was running things, except when he came face to face with the Most High God. When he recognized that the fire he had ordered to destroy the three men, who wouldn't worship his pagan gods,

Nature Spirituality

had preserved their lives, he was forced to concede that God was greater. The God of the three men had saved them from the flames, not even letting their hair be singed or their clothes scorched. They didn't even smell like smoke. Nebuchadnezzar may be second in command in his world, but the top position went to God.

Ironically, King Nebuchadnezzar, one of the most powerful men on the earth, becomes a believer in the God of the three Jewish men. In a letter to "the people of all nations and races on the earth" (Daniel 4:1), he wrote: "I am glad to tell about the wonderful miracles God Most High has done for me. His miracles are mighty and marvelous. He will rule forever, and his kingdom will never end" (Daniel 4:2–3).

The furnace-crematorium into which the three men were thrown is turned into a womb from which they are born again. It also becomes a womb from which the king emerges with faith in the God of the Jews. The fire intended to destroy ends up saving. God, as fire, wraps those who trust God in a water-soaked blanket of fiery love and protects them with saving grace.

> **Journal:** What experiences have you had of fire as a preservative rather than a destroyer? From what were you saved by God's fire? In what ways were you born again, given new life? How was your faith in God renewed or strengthened?
>
> **Prayer:** Most High God, you saved your faithful servants in the flames. Wrap me in the fire of your Holy Spirit. Quiet my fears and help me to trust more deeply in the teachings of your Son, Jesus Christ. You are exalted among the nations for ever and ever. Amen.

Destroying Fire

> **Scripture:** Listen, all of you! Earth and everything on it, pay close attention. The LORD God accuses you from his holy temple. And he will come down to crush underfoot every pagan altar. Mountains will melt beneath his feet like wax beside a fire. Valleys will vanish like water rushing down a ravine. This will happen because of the terrible sins of Israel, the descendants of Jacob (Micah 1:2–5a).

Fire

Reflection: What is the most horrible type of destruction that human beings can imagine? The answer is desolation by fire. We know that fire destroys whatever it touches. Put a container of wax near a fire and it will melt; if it is close enough, it will also burst into flames. Molten, fiery lava emerging from the depths of the earth through a volcano's vent turns to ash everything it covers. A raging forest fire burns every tree, blade of grass, and bush in its path. Houses, hotels, and office buildings are reduced to piles of rubble by fire.

It is no wonder that the Hebrew Bible (Old Testament) Book of Micah uses the image of fire to exhort the people of Samaria to turn away from their sins of idolatry and turn toward the God of Israel. If they don't realign themselves with God, the prophet threatens them with fiery destruction.

At one time the area called Samaria had been part of the kingdom of Israel. David had united the kingdoms of the north and the south into one. But after David's son, Solomon, the united empire was once again divided, each with its own king. To the Jews the Samaritans were a break-away group. The Samaritans had established their own temple for God on Mount Gerizim, which infuriated the Jews even more. Thus, the Samaritans were viewed as a detestable people by the Jews. They did not worship the real God of Israel, but built a rival temple and were worshiping pagan gods. Micah, of course from Judah, declares that Samaria will be destroyed by God's fire.

If God's fire is understood to be Sargon from Assyria, then the city was captured and thousands of the people deported early in the seventh century BCE. Once the area was captured by the Assyrians, it was settled with foreign peoples who had their own gods.

The destructive properties of fire are used by the author of the Christian Bible (New Testament) Book of Revelation to describe the triumph of good over evil. After writing about how God will defeat Satan, the author states: ". . . Fire will come down from heaven to destroy the whole army. Then the devil who fooled them will be thrown into the lake of fire and burning sulfur" (Revelation 20:9b–10a). All evil will be burned up in fire.

God's burning presence is experienced often enough. Personal biases are destroyed by consciences God sears with new understanding. When we know deep within ourselves what we ought to do but take a different path, fire often leaps up in front of us in the person of one who guides us where we prefer not to go. Those who turn away from drugs, alcohol, and sexual addictions and become advocates of the very system they once set out to overcome have had their former lives destroyed by the fire of recovery. The fire that destroys also renews. The land of Samaria was one of the first places the followers of Jesus of Nazareth preached, and the Samaritans believed in him. Sometimes, we need a destroying fire in order to experience the renewal that follows in its path.

Journal: When have you been destroyed by fire? Of what did it consist? What pagan god was destroyed? What evil was consumed by God's fire? How were you renewed?

Prayer: God of light, your gift of fire both purifies and renews. Send the fire of you Spirit upon all your people that they may be cleansed of all sin and filled with new life. Count me among those you have chosen through Jesus Christ, the Lord. Amen.

Baptized with Fire

Scripture: [John the Baptist said:] "I baptize you with water so that you will give up your sins. But someone more powerful is going to come, and I am not good enough even to carry his sandals. He will baptize you with the Holy Spirit and with fire" (Matthew 3:11).

Reflection: Using what biblical scholars call Q (from the German word "Quelle," meaning "source"), a no-longer extant collection of sayings of John the Baptist and Jesus, the author of Matthew's Gospel and the author of Luke's Gospel portray John the Baptist as saying that Jesus will baptize with the Holy Spirit and fire, while John baptizes with water in the Jordan River (cf. Luke 3:16). Neither author tells the reader of what baptism with the Holy Spirit and with fire consists. However, it is not difficult to determine when the whole of Matthew's Gospel is read and understood.

Matthew understands baptism with the Holy Spirit and with fire to refer to the judgment at the end of time. In its earliest days, Christianity was very apocalyptic, expecting Jesus' imminent return and the end of the world. Fire was used as an image to indicate what would happen to those who did not repent. Very likely, the author of Matthew's Gospel borrowed the idea from the prophet Isaiah, who, using similar language, told the Israelites: "You will go up in flames like straw and hay! You have rejected the teaching of the holy LORD God All-Powerful of Israel" (6:24ab). Likewise, the prophet Jeremiah warned the people by delivering God's word to them: ". . . I, the LORD all-Powerful, will flood Judah with my fiery anger until nothing is left—no people or animals, no trees or crops" (7:20). The author of Matthew's Gospel clarifies his use of fire in several places, warning the reader of the "danger of the fires of hell" (5:22), "the fire that never goes out" (18:8), and "the everlasting fire prepared for the devil" (25:41).

The author of the first gospel in the Christian Bible (New Testament) does not have a clearly defined pneumatology or understanding of the Holy Spirit. He mentions that Mary "learned that she was going to have a baby by God's Holy Spirit" (1:18) and that Joseph is told that "the baby that Mary will have is from the Holy Spirit" (1:20), but Matthew never defines who the Holy Spirit is nor states what its role is. Later in the gospel, the Matthean Jesus declares, ". . . If you speak against the Holy Spirit, you can never be forgiven, either in this life or in the life to come" (12:32), uniting the Holy Spirit to his fiery judgment theme. Finally, at the end of the gospel, the disciples are told to "Baptize . . . in the name of the Father, the Son, and the Holy Spirit," (28:19), a baptismal formula of the early church. However, here again there is no clearly defined understanding of the Holy Spirit.

Often, we don't understand how the Holy Spirit works fiery judgment either, but we have experienced that baptismal call which challenges us to evaluate our lives in relationship to the gospel. After buying something we didn't need, we may feel a fiery dart of guilt touch us. After wasting dollars gambling, we may see an angry spouse coming our way. Who hasn't gotten burnt in a relationship that was at best the use of the other person? Where there's fire, there's the Holy Spirit. Where there's the Holy Spirit, there's God—present, judging, and calling us to live the baptism we have received from Jesus: the Holy Spirit and fire.

JOURNAL: When have you recently felt like you were being judged with fire by God? At what end of time in your life did this take place? In what ways was the Holy Spirit prodding you? In what ways were you not living your baptismal promises?

PRAYER: Fiery God, you sent your Son, Jesus, to set the world on fire with your gift of the Holy Spirit. Baptize me in water and fire that I may continue Jesus' work all my days. I ask this in the name of him who is Lord for ever and ever. Amen.

Fiery Tongues

SCRIPTURE: On the day of Pentecost all the Lord's followers were together in one place. Suddenly there was a noise from heaven like the sound of a mighty wind! It filled the house where they were meeting. Then they saw what looked like fiery tongues moving in all directions, and a tongue came and settled on each person there. The Holy Spirit took control of everyone, and they began speaking whatever languages the Spirit let them speak (Acts 2:1–4).

REFLECTION: The anonymous author of Luke's Gospel is also the author of the Acts of the Apostles, which contains the account of two Pentecosts: the Jewish one above and the Gentile one later in the book (cf. Acts 10:44–48). The author never tells the reader who the Holy Spirit is, manifested as a mighty wind, fiery tongues, and myriad languages. However, it is not difficult to determine when the whole of Luke's Gospel is read and understood before beginning to read the Acts.

The author of Luke's Gospel has a well-developed pneumatology or theology of the Holy Spirit. He understands the role of the Holy Spirit, signified by fire, to guide the church. The Spirit is the force behind the events in God's plan for the world. Mary is told by the angel, "The Holy Spirit will come down to you, and God's power will come over you" (Luke 1:35). The Holy Spirit comes upon Elizabeth and she conceives John the Baptist, who has the "power of the Holy Spirit . . . with him from the time he is born" (Luke 1:15), and after his birth his father, Zechariah, is overcome with the Holy Spirit (cf. Luke 1:41, 67). The aged Simeon is directed by God's Spirit to go to the temple and meet the infant Jesus (cf. Luke 2:26–27).

". . . The Holy Spirit came down upon [Jesus]" (Luke 3:22) at the time of his baptism. Once Jesus is baptized, Luke writes, ". . . The power of the Holy Spirit was with him, and the Spirit led him into the desert" (4:1). In the synagogue on the Sabbath, Jesus reads the words "The Lord's Spirit has come to me" (Luke 4:18) from the prophet Isaiah. Luke tells the reader that "Jesus felt the joy that comes from the Holy Spirit" (Luke 10:21), and the Lucan Jesus tells his disciples, ". . . Your heavenly Father is . . . ready to give the Holy Spirit to anyone who asks" (Luke 11:13). However, anyone who speaks "against the Holy Spirit . . . cannot be forgiven" (Luke 12:10). The Holy Spirit continues to guide Jesus to his death, when his last words declare that he is returning the Spirit to his Father, who pours it out on his followers (cf. Luke 23:46). The Spirit who guides Jesus now guides the church.

In a unique monologue, Luke portrays Jesus as understanding his mission on earth as one of setting a fire. He says, "I came to set fire to the earth, and I wish it were already on fire!" (Luke 12:49). The earth is finally set on fire with Pentecost's fiery tongues. The Holy Spirit is God's presence which lights a fire under Jesus' disciples, helping them profess their faith in his resurrection, filling them with the breath of new life, and putting the words they need to speak on their lips. The Holy Spirit is the all-engulfing presence of God on earth.

In a way of speaking, Jesus is a pyromaniac in Luke's Gospel. He spreads the fire of God's presence, God's reign, wherever he goes and entrusts the mission of continuing to set the world on fire to his followers. Both the Jewish Pentecost and the Gentile event represent the fulfillment of John the Baptist's words concerning Jesus: "He will baptize you with the Holy Spirit and with fire" (Luke 3:16).

JOURNAL: In what ways have you experienced being filled with the Holy Spirit? How do you describe your experiences: as a mighty wind, a fiery tongue, speaking the right words? In what ways do you continue the mission of Jesus to set the world on fire with God's presence? In other words, what Holy Spirit fires have you set recently?

PRAYER: Father of Jesus, you sent your Holy Spirit to your Son's followers to form them into your church and to guide them through time. Pour out a fiery tongue on me, and enable me to bring the good news of salvation to all I meet. Hear this prayer through Jesus Christ, the Lord. Amen.

Nature Spirituality

Fiery Anger

SCRIPTURE: Jerusalem, city of David, the place of my altar, you are in for trouble! I will surround you and prepare to attack from all sides. From deep in the earth, you will call out for help with only a faint whisper. Then your cruel enemies will suddenly be swept away like dust in a windstorm. I, the LORD All-Powerful, will come to your rescue with a thundering earthquake and a fiery whirlwind. Every brutal nation that attacks Jerusalem and makes it suffer will disappear like a dream when night is over (Isaiah 29:1, 3–7).

REFLECTION: Does God get angry? The answer to the question is both yes and no. Yes, God gets angry from a human point of view. The Hebrew Bible (Old Testament) Book of Isaiah makes that clear: "The LORD will get furious. His fearsome voice will be heard, his arm will be seen ready to strike, and his anger will be like a destructive fire, followed by thunderstorms and hailstones" (30:30). As seen from our limited perspective, the Holy One gets angry at God's people and the Mighty One gets angry at their enemies.

However, the answer to "Does God get angry?" is also "No." To attribute anger to God brings down the All-powerful Deity to a human level. God, by definition, is beyond the human emotion of anger. To say that God gets angry is to diminish God's supremacy and create God in human likeness. What ancient peoples labeled as "God's anger" is their name for their experience of not following God's ways and the problems which resulted. For example, when the Israelites broke the covenant, their borders were invaded by their enemies. They attributed the invasion to God's anger with them.

Jesus, the incarnate Son of God, demonstrated anger. All of the gospels contain a story about Jesus cleansing the temple after triumphantly entering Jerusalem (cf. Mark 11:15–19, Matthew 21:12–13, Luke 19:45–48, and John 2:13–22). Jesus sets free the sheep and the cattle being sold in the temple and turns over the tables of the money-changers. His anger at turning the sign of God's presence—the Temple—into a marketplace motivates him to action.

While we may not always be aware of it, we, too, experience God's anger. When we recognize an injustice done, such as a member of our family falsely accused by another, and speak about it, we are sharing in God's

Fire

anger. Contributing to our favorite charity in order to help those who have no food, no home, and no clothes can be an act of God's anger at an economic system that rewards a few at the expense of many. Becoming aware that the legal system may be controlled by those who have the funds to buy the best of lawyers may cause God's anger to arise within us.

God's fiery anger is not something that God does to us on the outside, such as attacking us with the fury of thunderstorms or hailstorms or permitting our enemies to invade the borders of our country—although, we may prefer to describe it in those ways. God's anger rises up as a manifestation of God's presence in people, like it did in Jesus of Nazareth, and we cannot hold back. Like a fire within us, we know we must speak about our moral, economic, and legal failures, call ourselves and others to conversion, and focus on the God who fires our anger to begin with. When we do that, we experience God rescuing us with fiery grace.

Journal: What type of moral injustice has caused God's anger to flare up in you? What type of economic injustice has caused God's anger to flare up in you? What type of legal injustice has caused God's anger to flare up in you? In what ways have you experienced God's anger, shared it with others, and sparked changes? What is your greatest fear when you reflect on God's fiery anger?

Prayer: All-powerful Lord, your anger arouses justice, care for the homeless, and food for the hungry. Stir up the fire of your anger in me that I may be a devoted follower of Jesus Christ, your Son, who lives with you and the Holy Spirit, one God for ever and ever. Amen.

Hell's Fire

Scripture: Jesus said to his disciples: ". . . If your hand causes you to sin, cut it off! You would be better off to go into life crippled than to have two hands and be thrown into the fires of hell that never go out. If your foot causes you to sin, chop it off. You would be better off to go into life lame than to have two feet and be thrown into hell. If you eye causes you to sin, get rid of it. You would be better off to go into God's kingdom with only one eye than to have two eyes and be thrown into hell. The worms there never die, and the fire never stops burning" (Mark 9:43, 45, 47–48).

Nature Spirituality

REFLECTION: While the author of Mark's Gospel may be the first Christian Bible (New Testament) author to mention hell, he does not develop it as much as does the author of Matthew's Gospel, who, using Mark's Gospel, enhanced his own. In his first mention of hell, Matthew portrays Jesus as saying: "If your right eye causes you to sin, poke it out and throw it away. It is better to lose one part of your body, than for your whole body to end up in hell. If your right hand causes you to sin, chop it off and throw it away! It is better to lose one part of your body, than for you whole body to be thrown into hell" (Matthew 5:29–30).

Later in his gospel, Matthew employs the material he borrowed from Mark's Gospel concerning hell. He portrays Jesus as saying to his disciples: "If your hand or foot causes you to sin, chop it off and throw it away! You would be better off to go into life crippled or lame than to have two hands or two feet and be thrown into the fire that never goes out. If your eye causes you to sin, poke it out and get rid of it. You would be better off to go into life with only one eye than to have two eyes and be thrown into the fires of hell" (Matthew 18:8–9).

Matthew also contains one saying of Jesus about hell which parallels one found in Luke's Gospel, indicating that both authors had access to Q, a hypothetical source of sayings. The Matthean Jesus says: "Don't be afraid of people. They can kill you, but they cannot harm your soul. Instead, you should fear God who can destroy both your body and your soul in hell" (Matthew 10:28). The Lukan Jesus declares: "My friends, don't be afraid of people. They can kill you, but after that, there is nothing else they can do. God is the one you must fear. Not only can he take your life, but he can throw you into hell. God is certainly the one you should fear!" (Luke 12:4–5).

In a unique reference, Jesus accuses the Pharisees and teachers of the Law of Moses of winning a follower and making "that person twice as fit for hell" (Matthew 23:15) as they are. Later, he calls them snakes and asks, "How can you escape going to hell?" (Matthew 23:33)

Every reference to hell in Mark, Matthew, and Luke is a translation of the Greek word "Gehenna," which was not originally a reference to a state in the afterlife, but referred to a valley outside of the city of Jerusalem. Gehenna was the ancient site of a shrine to a pagan god where human sacrifice was offered. Hence, there is the reference to the fire. At one time, it also seems to have become the city's garbage dump, where the worms never die. With this background, Jesus' references to hell in the gospels becomes not only a non-desirable place to be, but Jesus implies that those who fail to give up everything—even a body part—for the reign of God are not even good garbage! The understanding of hell as a fiery "place" in the afterlife was gradually developed by Christian theologians who came to understand God in terms of human justice, rewarding the righteous and punishing the wicked.

The point of the various stories is this: God controls what is going on. The rule of God encompasses everything and everyone. There is no place to which people can escape from God's reign—even the fiery garbage dump! To recognize that God is God and we are humans, creatures, means that we have a healthy fear of the Creator, who wants to include us in God's realm. We are exhorted by the gospels to give all that is necessary to share in God's domain, which even encompasses Gehenna, hell, the garbage dump.

JOURNAL: What is your image, picture, understanding of hell? What is the role of fire in your image, picture, understanding? What unlikely fiery places have you discovered God? In what ways did those experiences help you to become a better human being in God's domain?

PRAYER: God of power and might, from your heavenly temple you examine what your people do on earth. With your Spirit direct their daily actions. Guide me in the footsteps of Jesus Christ, your Son, who is Lord for ever and ever. Amen.

Post-resurrection Fire

SCRIPTURE: When the disciples got out of the boat, they saw some bread and a charcoal fire with fish on it. Jesus told his disciples, "Bring some of the fish you just caught." Simon Peter got back into the boat and dragged the net to shore. Jesus said, "Come and eat!" But none of the disciples dared ask who he was. They knew he was the Lord. Jesus took the bread in his hands and gave some of it to his disciples. He did the same with the fish. This was the third time that Jesus appeared to his disciples after he was raised from death (John 21:9–11a, 12–14).

REFLECTION: It is no Johannine accident that the story of Jesus' third post-resurrection appearance to his disciples includes bread, fish, and fire.

Nature Spirituality

In the appendix or later addition (chapter 21) to John's Gospel, Jesus, God's fire, continues to burn with divine luminosity. He has been raised from the dead. The author of the story, using several signs easily recognized by early Jewish-Christian believers, proclaims that God, in the person of Jesus of Nazareth, is present with people.

The third appearance of Jesus heralds a theophany, a presence of God. The Jewish passover, a celebration of Israel's imminent death before Pharaoh's approaching army and the people's escape through the Sea of Reeds—the way God gave life to them—became the meal celebrating the new passover, Jesus' death and resurrection to new life. Using the elements of the Passover—namely, bread and wine—those first believers in the resurrection found a way to proclaim that God had saved people again through Jesus' escape from death. Thus, Jesus' breaking of breakfast bread and sharing it with his disciples is a proclamation of his death and resurrection, or eucharist, another of God's theophanies.

The use of fish in the narrative should not be missed. Those first followers of Jesus had been inept fishermen. By following Jesus, they became good at their trade—catching an abundance of believers through their proclamation of their faith in God's latest theophanic passover. In the story in John's Gospel, they bring their catch to Jesus, who serves them his passover meal. In other words, once people profess faith and are led to Christ, the disciples get out of the way and let the risen one feed them with his passover food.

The charcoal fire is not merely a ring of stones with flames leaping from its center and cooking fish for breakfast. It is the fire of resurrection, the fire of life, the fire of God. Jesus, the prophet from Nazareth, burns like fire with eternal life. He lights up the minds and hearts of his disciples, of those who dare to believe that he is the new passover lamb, and of the world. Jesus glows with God's fire. He burns with a divine luminosity that draws fishermen to recognize that God is present in him and as him in human flesh.

The historical Jesus of Nazareth has become the Christ of faith who continues to shed the light of his fire upon the world. We can recognize it in the unity of those surrounding a campfire, sharing roasted marshmallows and drinking apple cider. We discover it in front of the fireplace as the members of a family share their day with each other, snacking on cookies and milk. And, of course, the Easter Vigil fire, kindled in the darkness only one night a year, unites the assembly into one fiery procession, as the fire

Fire

ignites the Easter candle and it shares the flame with everyone. Christ our light has died and is risen. We are dead and risen through baptism. We await final death and fiery, eternal life.

JOURNAL: What experiences have you had of God's fire, the presence of Jesus, with other people? For each experience, identify what food and drink were shared, what physical or emotional fire was present, and what death and new life resulted. What other signs of God's presence were there in each of your experiences? How can the annual Easter Vigil fire be a celebration for you of all your other experiences of God's fire?

PRAYER: God of resurrection, the fire of your Holy Spirit raised Jesus from the dead and filled him with eternal life. Lead me with the fire of your love throughout my life, that after my death I may one day share in the resurrection of him who is Lord for ever and ever. Amen.

www.ingramcontent.com/pod-product-compliance
Lightning Source LLC
Chambersburg PA
CBHW050828160426
43192CB00010B/1941